With best
wishes to
Nancy O'Malley -
Perhaps this book
will inspire you to
your talents & get some
of your own stories in P.

Nan Schram Williams
11/8/73

Writing and Selling
the Personal Story

A COMPREHENSIVE GUIDE

confess
for profit

by Nan Schram Williams

Douglas-West Publishers, Inc.
Los Angeles, California

To my mother, Anna Schram
To my husband, Orval Dupree
And to our children, Dick, Anne, and Jim
    in appreciation for love and understanding.

Library of Congress Catalogue Card Number 72—92133
ISBN 0—913264—09—1

Published 1973 by
Douglas-West Publishers, Inc.,
Los Angeles, California
and printed in the United States.

ACKNOWLEDGMENT

Acknowledgment is made, with thanks, to those several editors who guided my early efforts and have granted permission to use excerpts from published stories in this book; also to those established writers who gave me generous assistance as a novice and have granted permission to use incidents from their experiences and stories as examples of methods and procedures.

PREFACE

Almost everyone has a story to tell.

It may be a dramatic experience which has deeply affected his or her life in a material or emotional way, or might have changed it altogether. Most people at one time or another are beset by personal or family or business problems which involve deep emotions. The nature of such problems may derive from various situations, incidents or disturbing events in the home or in the office.

At these times, everyone needs someone to talk to; someone to whom he or she can "spill over," bring the matter out into the open and find its solution. Often this is not possible with a member of one's family or friends; even a minister or doctor. To do so might prove so embarrassing as to create a psychosis of deep guilt or fear or shame.

Confession magazines today provide this much-needed outlet for both reader and writer.

Writing one's story almost always brings relief to a confused and troubled mind, eases the heartache resulting from loss of a loved one, or deep sorrow of various kinds and origins, and very frequently helps the writer to find comfort or solutions to emotional problems.

Reading stories about emotional problems of others which may be similar to their own often helps readers cope with their own problems and find satisfactory solutions to them.

It is for the thousands of troubled human beings, young and old, who need to unburden their minds and hearts to someone, that this book has been written. In it I have endeavored to direct the nonprofessional writer in the craft of setting down his or her story on paper in a professional manner by using proper techniques of the writing craft. The writer may be a homemaker, a career woman, a misunderstood husband or wife, a confused young woman or man seeking emotional answers to life.

Established writers who may have taken time out from writing careers to raise a family also should find this book helpful as a "refresher course" in reviewing the basic rules and updating new trends and flexible rules of the profession. Each generation brings about some changes in contemporary acceptable usage; trends which fit the times.

The writer of the confession-type story (or personal problem story) must be aware not only of his or her particular world, but to some extent the world of friends and neighbors. He must be able to probe his or her own beliefs and philosophies concerning success, failure, love, sex and marriage, and many other kinds of involvement which all must share: racial, political and religious. I have endeavored to offer writers a realistic and professional method for achieving better understanding of themselves and those people who make up their lives.

In my work with individual writers and class groups, I have found that writing techniques frequently can be explained more clearly by means of a step-by-step analysis of a published story. This method helps the new writer select and identify those elements which make up most stories, and organize these to create an interesting and convincing story which is both readable and saleable—if sales are the writer's objective. For obvious reasons, I have used my own published stories for this purpose, except in two instances which involved stories by others who granted me permission to use them.

In selecting stories for analysis, I have chosen some from each general viewpoint-category: male, female, teenager, adult. Also a variety of experiences from as broad a strata of life as is possible to handle in one volume.

It is my earnest hope that readers will find this book helpful toward developing his or her own writing potential, and perhaps in some special way, also inspiring.

Nan Schram Williams

1

DEFINITIONS: The Confession Story

"I want to confess!" you say to your priest, minister, doctor, your best friend or your mother. "I *must* confess. I have to get this terrible thing off my mind. Let me tell you what really happened!"

Thousands of people everywhere have felt this inner cry whether or not they expressed it in those words. Confession *is* good for the soul.

But what is it you want to confess? What has given you a guilt complex? Would you answer these questions in one of the following ways or with something equivalent to them?

"My wife was an alcoholic . . . ."

"I discovered I was a test-tube baby . . . ."

"I pretended I was a prostitute to get even with my mother . . . ."

"I accused my child of killing her brother . . . ."

"I got my high-school sweetheart pregnant . . . ."

"My husband was a child molester . . . ."

"I hated God when I found I was a Negro . . . ."

The list of reasons for the need to confess is endless. Almost everyone has a problem of one kind or another; emotional or personal conflicts which affect their lives but which cannot be discussed with family or friends. And their need to confess becomes stronger from day to day.

So why not confess? Confess for profit! *Write* your story and sell it to one of the confession magazines which pay well for personal problem stories. You will benefit emotionally from writing it—confessing on paper—and you may be helping someone else who reads your story and who has a similar problem.

A secret is a secret only if you can tell it to someone. Whether you talk about it or write about it, the guilt complex, the worry and fear locked away in your mind because of that secret are relieved, perhaps will vanish altogether. This is the purpose of psychiatrists—to listen patiently while you dig deeply into your subconscious for those secrets which have caused your inhibitions and frustrations and anxieties. Many psychoanalyists ask their patients to write out the problem at the end of each session.

You can do this without consulting a psychiatrist. Get rid of your guilty secrets—and get paid for doing so.

The purpose of this book is to show you how to write your "personal problem" (confession) story in a manner acceptable to magazines that buy such stories. It makes little difference whether you are young or old, male or female, wife, husband, grandmother or grandfather, or a mother-in-law, the confession magazine's "confessional" is open to all. A study of the instructions in this book will help you to tell your stories in such a way that the reader is able to understand *your* problem or heartbreak and consequently is better able to understand his or her own problems or disappointments.

The first check any writer receives usually provides incentive to write more stories. If this happens to you, whether your story is true or fictional, the rules of writing, the general techniques, are much the same and you will find them in this book.

The confession story market is made up of some twenty-five individual magazines published by a comparatively small number of chain-magazine groups. It is perhaps the largest magazine market in terms of the number of manuscripts purchased each month, with circulation running into the millions of copies sold each month.

This vast human interest story market is wide open to new writers.

Editors of these magazines must have a steady supply of stories and these come for the most part from writers who have lived them. The pay for acceptable stories is excellent. (A comprehensive listing of these magazines will be given later.)

Confession magazine editors want stories about young love, courtship, marriage, children, infidelity, frustrated love, divorce; in short, stories that run the gamut of human emotion and experience. These stories, of course, must be exciting and provocative, yet told with realism and conviction.

One top-market editor has defined the confession story as "a believable story told in the first person, reflecting the ordinary emotional conflicts of ordinary people. The narrator is the central character around whom action and drama center."

When writing your own personal problem story *you* become the central character, the narrator.

Another editor's advice to new writers states, "An acceptable story is one about real people directed to an audience of very real people." It is a good rule to keep in mind. Write your own story with honesty and conviction, as you would tell it to someone you are sure will understand. For that is the audience of story-readers all across America, and most of these readers have similar problems.

"Sex," one editor has emphasized, "is definitely a necessary ingredient in every story but never included merely for the sake of sensationalism. When it is introduced into a story, it must be an integral and significant part of the problem which confronts the individual; the cause of the problem or some tragedy resulting from that problem. Dramatic writing is important, in fact demanded. But don't go overboard in this. Don't 'spread it on so thick' you destroy believability. Such writing, in editorial language, is called "purple prose," and is a fault that can earn you a rejection slip, not the check you hope for."

One of this writer's stories, which was published in *Personal Romances*, is an example of how you can tell a very dramatic story while avoiding purple prose. "My Little Girl's Letter to God" is analyzed later in this book.

Most confession magazines include "man-told" stories; that is, stories told from the male viewpoint. These may be stories by a husband, male lover, or teenage boy. The important point in male- or female-told stories is to mirror life as it is being lived in today's world; stick to the problem and avoid getting sidetracked. Many writers try to include everything even if it means going off on tangents, thinking such sideline events make their story more realistic and dramatic. On the contrary. You merely distract the reader's mind from the main story—*your* story.

Dramatizing incidents and emotions in your story is very important. This is best achieved by creating a scene with dialogue between your characters. But be sure to keep the dialogue natural, the way people really talk; the scenes as people behave in times of crisis, times of despair, discouragement, shock, anger, devotion—the whole list of possible reactions to unusual events.

When you decide to write your own story, first try to recall the scenes and happenings at the time the problem arose. Use the dialogue you used or something as close to it as possible. Try to reproduce the feelings you experienced at the time—anger, joy, hatred, humiliation.

Right here let me make an important comment about personal-experience stories.

If you have a feeling of shame toward confession magazines, either about reading them or writing for them, get rid of that feeling! There is no basis for it. Today's confession magazines are designed to help men and women solve those problems which torment them and jeopardize success and happiness, by "talking them out" on paper, or through reading about problems similar to their own and finding the direction needed to solve them. In small towns or isolated areas, it is often impossible to have personal contact with others without sacrificing your personal privacy. Everyone knows everyone else's business! For these readers the confession magazine provides much the same kind of advice and counsel a psychiatrist, or the family doctor, minister or marriage counselor would give if the distraught person could seek or afford such help.

Twenty-five years ago, confession magazines were banned by churches, moral uplift societies, and most parents. A young girl locked herself in the bathroom or the woodshed while reading this "forbidden trash," and secretly passed the magazine among her friends who went through the same secrecy until the magazine was worn out. Yet the stories, then as now, were basically true. Many were the honest outpourings of human beings in trouble, with no one to talk to about them.

Fortunately, present times and people have changed. So, to some extent, has the format of the confession story, although the markets for such stories remain constant and lucrative.

At their inception the confession story usually followed a pattern often referred to as "sin-suffer-and-repent." The emphasis then was on shocking events, the more sordid aspects of life. Readers found excitement in reading them, but few answers to their own problems. Readers of such stories at that time were largely the underprivileged working girls, love-starved waitresses and housemaids, store clerks—all with little or no excitement in their daily lives which were so often confined to dull routines. They read confession magazines for escape, and for momentary erotic thrills.

After World War II, there were almost immediately drastic changes in economy, education and moral values; and vast change in the living and working conditions of the average man and woman and their families. There was also a change in reading habits. Magazines began to change, covering much wider fields of interest. A greater variety of magazines began to emerge. More people could afford to buy and read them. Education expanded into all areas of America. Most young housewives in rural communities, farm boys and girls, underprivileged city and small town children now had at least a high-school education or its equivalent. Television is available to most families however isolated the town or community, or limited the financial conditions may be. Consequently, new standards of living have emerged; the average individual's horizons have widened. The readers of confession magazines today expect and get stories on a level with their own improved social, educational, and financial conditions. Stories about *this* generation's average person, not those isolated situations which excited readers of the pre-war era.

This is undoubtedly true of your own life today.

You have learned to carry on, cope, endure, or seek new ways and experiences. You have grown up mentally and benefitted from life experiences, whether your problem was one of drinking, narcotic addiction, adultery, sexual permissiveness, disrespect for your parents, or rebellion against conformity to the social customs. Or believing the world owed you a living and you were going to collect no matter who got in the way!

Most of these experiences have been turning points in your life. Turning points frequently create conflicts and challenges. They are also the stuff from which stories are made.

Recognize these periods for what they are or were, add the necessary ingredients of dialogue, dramatization and an organized format, and you have a marketable confession story, a story which fits the new pattern for such stories: "Sin, suffer, repent and *vindicate*."

It is that moment when you made an "about face," determined to change your ways and make up for your mistakes, which today's reader wants to hear about. Often it is also the kind of story you are keeping locked up in your own mind and heart, afraid to talk about even to your closest friends. *Write that story!* It may offer readers, as well as yourself, new hope, inspiration and courage; the way out of a dilemma they may be facing without the encouragement needed to make that "about face," and change their own life for the better. The solution you found may also be a solution the reader has been seeking— perhaps a young husband, a teenager, a troubled young wife and mother whose husband is serving our country far from home. You can, with concentration and real effort, learn how to tell your story and perhaps stories of others with problems, and receive sizeable checks for your endeavor, if you want or need to earn, or want only to unburden your mind and heart of sorrow or guilt or the aftermath of some great tragedy in your life.

But let me now sound an important warning.

Editors do not look favorably on stories which read like sermons. They do not want you to shout about the hellfire-and-brimstone that await all sinners. However, they *do* want stories which present a *moral;* a recognizable *reason* for telling your story in the first place. And this point, or moral, must be proved by the conclusion of your story. I was fortunate to have William Lindsay Gresham, author of *Nightmare Alley, Limbo Tower,* and the cele-brated biography of *Houdini.;* as a dear friend and neighbor in a New York suburb. I had met him shortly after I began trying to sell some of the stories I had been laboring over for several years. He had been an editor of "pulp" magazines while contributing to the top general magazines: the *Post*, *Colliers*, *Esquire*, and many others which were popular in the 40s and 50s but are no longer published. He had turned to novel writing as high-paying magazines were discontinued.

Bill read my first novel attempt, a work of some seventy thousand words, using first-person narrative. It was a wartime love story concerning a sweetheart, a son and a husband, and I'd given it "my all."

"Knock off novel writing for a while," he advised. "Write some short fiction. There's a bigger market right now for it."

I argued, "Why do you say that? Your wife has just sold her novel *Gaspe Bay* after two years sending it from editor to editor and gathering rejection slips." (His wife was professionally known as Joy Davidman.)

"Because you're not ready for novel writing. Try the confession market, Nan. You know how to make your characters come alive. You might start by turning your novel into a novelette for that market."

The very thought of using *my* talents for confession magazines shocked me.

"Bill, how could you!" I moaned. "Even if I sold some stories to that market I'd be ashamed to tell anyone." I felt as most of my family and friends did then who had never read a confession magazine.

Bill pinned me down. "Have you read any of those magazines, Nan?" I admitted I hadn't.

"Then read some of them. If you intend to be a writer

you need to know your markets. Writing is a business, not just a career. You need to earn from it."

"But what about sex? I couldn't . . . ."

"If sex belongs in the story, use it. If it doesn't, don't. It's that simple." He then explained the difference between love-sex and rape-sex; and that while some editors used stories with some pretty lurid sex in the plotting, most stories dealt with natural, deeply emotional romantic love scenes. Listening to him gave me a brand new slant on writing, and a very different attitude toward confession magazines.

I bought two or three of them, still feeling a little "sneaky," read them carefully, and found that Bill was right; these were human stories about very human people in one kind of trouble or another—the kinds of troubles most people experience occasionally.

Convinced now that I could handle my story with more realism and write emotional scenes without ugliness, I reread my novel. How could I cut down 70,000 words to about 17,500 words, which was the average length then for a novelette?

"Concentrate on one major problem," Bill advised. "The girl calling herself a war-widow to protect her illegitimate child from stigma, marries. Then, a few years later she discovers that the sweetheart is still alive but maimed or permanently injured in the war. She has to make a decision: either to stay with her present husband and keep her secret, or tell the father of her child the truth and expose herself and the child. She is torn with indecision but finally decides to get a divorce and marry the child's father."

"Maybe that's not the way it happened," I protested.

"So, who cares? It makes a good story. An editor

doesn't expect all confession stories to be the absolute truth but they must convince the reader that they are. And it will if you give the story a strong moral reason for being written in the first place. That's built in in your novelette's theme, Nan: True love never dies."

Personally, I did not believe that philosophy, but for the sake of my story I set about developing the theme around the one-and-only-lifetime-love, with first-person telling.

Bill approved the story when it was finished and suggested I send it to *Modern Romances*. They accepted it, but wanted to talk with me about a change in the opening. I went to New York City and met my first real-life editor. To my amazement, I learned that the story was already scheduled for an early issue and I was shown the beautiful two-page center color illustration. But they'd changed the title to "Take Back My Wedding Ring." I was pleased; it made *me* want to read the story, so it would surely make their readers react the same way.

The editor explained the changes required. They seemed fairly simple. During my train ride home (a two-hour trip) I pencilled in the changes on the proofsheets the editor had given me, typed new pages that night, and mailed them the next morning. Two weeks later I received a check for $680.00.

Here is another warning to keep in mind:

When an editor asks for a change in a script, change *only that part.* Do *not* try to rewrite the whole story. Editors have told me that too often when a script that required one or two simple changes is returned for second reading, the parts which interested them originally have been so completely changed they scarcely recognize the manuscript as the same story. This is a fault in which beginning writers are inclined to indulge. For instance, suppose an editor has asked you to change Aunt Minnie into a kinder, more compassionate person. Instead of doing just that, you start thinking that maybe Uncle Louie ought to be meaner, or maybe you should let him get killed in an automobile accident. Pretty soon you have so "improved" your story it is sure to be rejected. The editor *liked* Uncle Louie the way he was.

When I received the check for my first sale to *Modern Romances* I telephoned my mother, excited and jubilant.

"But you won't be able to tell any one in the family or my friends, Mom," I warned her. "It's to be in a confession magazine."

"Did you get paid for it, Nan?"

"Of course. Six hundred and eighty dollars!"

Her response was one I shall remember the rest of my life, and I pass it on to you as a piece of good wisdom.

"If anyone is willing to pay you *that* much money for what you have to say, I'm proud of you." Then she asked, "What are you going to do with the money?"

"I haven't decided yet."

"You'd better frame it, Nan. A writer's first sale is something to remember."

I didn't promise to do that. I had my eye on a new car and the amount of my first check was just about enough for the down payment.

Encouraged by the sale I rescued some of my short stories from the bottom desk drawer and showed one of them, "Four Hearts and a Horse," to Bill. It ran about five thousand words and was written in third person, and had been rejected by several markets. The general plot was about two teenage boys and girls who were interested in horseback riding. One girl wanted the other girl's boy-friend, and managed to get him by causing an accident on the bridle path.

"Put it in first person," Bill advised, "and give it a moral which proves something. Maybe let the selfish girl reach a turning point in her life, and now realize the wrong she has done her friend. Handle it that way and I think you'll sell it."

I decided to revise the plot a little. Let the setting be a horse show instead of a bridle path encounter, and let the girl cheat to win a ribbon. Then later, when her conscience began to bother her, she confesses her wrong doing. In other words, she *vindicated* herself and ultimately, because of this honesty, wins the young man she is in love with after all. There were no big romantic scenes in this partic-ular story; just exciting competition.

The revised story was novelette length because it *needed* greater length to tell the story convincingly. Beware of "padding" a story for the sake of more length because it will bring a higher price on a per-word basis. Such methods are more likely to get you rejection slips than larger checks.

Again I submitted my story to *Modern Romance*, and was rewarded with a check. It was a big boost to my confidence, and gave me the desire to find more time for my writing and to work harder at it. Time to write, if you are a housewife with duties that must come first, or a career woman with a full-time time job, is not easy to come by. Often you have to *make* time for other ambi-tions, and usually this can be done by organizing your work and yourself, and working harder at writing in what-ever time you can manage for it.

But there are basic rules to be followed to reach your goals: a deep desire to be a writer, a willingness to accept professional criticism (such as my friend, Bill, gave me), and to revise or rewrite completely if necessary. Take pride in your work but don't treasure every golden word you put on paper as if it were indispensible. What to leave out of a story may be as important as what to put in. Nevertheless, there are a few definable ingredients which your story must have:

Reader Identification. This is of primary importance and one of the basic elements in confession or personal problem stories; also the first thing an editor looks for when selecting stories for acceptance. It means telling your story so convincingly that the reader feels a kinship with the main character; that is, *identifies* with him or her. Thus you prove a theory, teach a lesson, guide or advise, and often inspire the reader who may have a similar problem.

Main Character Selection. It is imperative in stories of this type that your main character be an average kind of person. Don't make him or her a movie star, a big-shot stock broker, or an exotic person of any kind, thinking it will add glamor to your story. Since the main character is "I," and the narration is in first person (to the reader, you) do not describe yourself as too beautiful, too handsome, exceptionally ugly or fat or thin, tall or short *unless* specific physical appearance is one of the problems or plot-developing elements of your story. For instance, if the story deals with a marriage about to break up because the wife became too fat, or the husband got too sloppy, then emphasize the physical appearance that indicates behavior. With the "villain" in the story you have wider latitude. He or she should be described in considerable detail. He is the "guy who did you wrong," or she is the gal who cheated on you, or the nosy mother-in-law who ruined your marriage. The reader must *identify* with these characters somewhat in reverse; that is, like or dislike as the story plot demands.

The main character in all confession stories must also command reader sympathy. This, despite the wrong-doing or "sin" he or she is about to reveal in the story. This "sin" may be stealing, cheating, unfaithfulness, alcoholism or drug abuse, even in some cases murder, but it is still the writer's task to present him in a sympathetic light; driven to these wrong-doings by actions of others. Such background details can be covered through what is termed "flashback sequences" which are explained in detail later in this book (page 000). But watch out that you don't let flashback scenes become prolonged to the point of digression from your main story.

Narrator Must Always Be Vindicated. This is achieved through plot development, by making the reader understand and approve the narrator's determination to right the wrongs committed against someone else, or to right a wrong done to him or her. Therefore the story must always end on an upbeat note; perhaps an inspiring solution to the problem which will also give the reader the courage to face his or her own problems.

Race and Religion. Never use differences of race, color or religion in an argumentative or derogative manner. If your story deals with either of these in its main theme (and many people have such stories to write), plot the story so that prejudice is overcome, lessons learned about brotherhood and good neighborliness or a hundred other positive approaches which will give universal meaning and inspiration to other readers.

Viewpoint. One of the most important rules of writing this kind of story is to keep the story flowing *through the mind and actions of the narrator.* Do *not* switch abruptly to the thoughts of another character in the story. For instance, if the narrator has visited the home of her closest girlfriend whose parents did not approve the friendship because of snobbery over some point, the narrator (you) can describe her reactions to the home and parents but cannot tell the reader what the parents thought of their daughter's best friend. If it is a favorable (surprise) reaction this can be indicated through the narrator's next meeting with her friend and their conversation. Emotions of others can only be explained through their effect upon, or the dialogue of, the narrator. Remember this simple rule: *the narrator is the eyes and mind of the reader.*

Make Your Story Believable. Fact is often stranger than fiction. On the other hand, a true story more often than not needs a little help from fiction; in other words, dramatizing with a dash of "literary license." The main events of the story may be very dramatic in themselves, but sometimes they may be too involved as they actually happened to relate without much digression into side paths. Change the keynote if necessary, as I was able to do in the story about the teenagers who loved horses; using a horse show instead of the bridle path where the real story happened. Also, the real-life ending to your story might not have been as conclusive or inspiring as the ending to your story must be. Here is where true creative writing comes in; where imagination and ingenuity play their part.

Emotion and Sex. This element has been touched upon earlier in this book, but can be expanded here. Emotion may build into a sex situation, but you must have a story reason for letting this happen. Sex must never be "dragged in" for the sake of sensationalism or shock, or to stir erotic reactions in the reader. And *never* use vulgar or obscene language. A good writer learns how to *imply* ugliness without using ugly words, where ugliness of any kind is an integral part of your story which it may well be. Do not depend entirely on these sordid elements, however; balance them, if they are a part of the story, with the gentleness or thoughtfulness of another character.

Theme and Structure. Every story must have a theme which usually involves two opposing philosophies. These create both the problem with which the story is concerned, and its ultimate solution or outcome. Confession stories particularly are largely based on argument between two different viewpoints; the right and wrong of behavior or thinking on the part of average people. One or the other viewpoint will win. You must decide before you start your story which viewpoint will win. Suppose you have been accused of something that is wrong which you did not do. Justice against injustice. Justice must triumph and you, the narrator, must be vindicated of wrong doing. The body of the story, therefore, is concerned with what the false accusation did to you emotionally, businesswise, etc., and what was done to bring about justice and truth. In the confession story, the narrator must always be a victim of either his own, or another's wrong doing, or simply a circumstance of life over which he or she has no control. Do not, however, depend upon "fate" or any supernatural event, or coincidence to solve the narrator's problem. And do *not* resort to gory automobile accidents, tear-jerking suicides, poisonings, shootings and other "gimmicks" to dispose of evil or unwanted characters; or victims of injustice or wrong-doing. If these are a bona-fide part of your story—any one of these tragedies—then build them into the plot and structure of your story with conviction and sufficient realism without wallowing in it for the sake of shocking the reader. Tragedy is a part of most people's lives to one degree or another. But these must be presented with restraint and purpose, always reaching toward compassion even if it is the villain who meets an untimely end of some kind.

Theme Vehicle. Every personal problem story has a theme vehicle character whether that person plays a prominent or subordinate part in the story itself. This person is one who advises, guides, or influences your main character in significant ways. However a vehicle character never becomes a protagonist of the main character, never fights or argues although he may try to reason with the main character.

A theme vehicle character may be a friend or relative or neighbor, male or female. His or her helpfulness may be premeditated with good intentions, or may be the result of some casual remark well meant but with no deep concern for the main character one way or the other. Often a remark more critical than sympathetic may influence the main character to "see himself as others see him", and so change his ways or actions for the better.

In most confession stories, however, the theme vehicle character is sympathetic to the main character and stands for the same principles and philosophies. His or her helpfulness comes from deep concern for the main characters—

one or both—in the story and in subtle ways may prepare the reader for the outcome of the story without destroying suspense by revealing it prematurely.

The Proper Use of Words and Devices. Nothing is duller than a "wordy" manuscript. The kind of writing that goes on and on, using three adjectives or adverbs where one would have carried more impact for the reader; or wandering off down "memory's lane" reciting incidents which have no bearing on the story you are attempting to write. Such overwriting obscures rather than portrays. Use descriptive words when needed and select them carefully. One strong word is more powerful than three or four mild words; but there is always *the right word* or two to portray what you want to say.

A story does not have to start at the beginning. More often than not chronological narration will become so boring to the reader he'll never finish the story. The device which is most often used is to open your story at some dramatic high point and then "flash back" to how it all began once you have seized the reader's interest.

These basic rules and suggestions will enable you to select the story you want to write based on your own experiences, and to "get it down on paper." That is, in "first draft." Stories, like children, grow through many stages. Don't be afraid to start, setting the story down much as you would tell it to a friend. From this first draft, and probably several subsequent drafts, you will polish and prune until there emerges a strong, convincing story with emotional impact and universal elements of courage, inspiration, understanding and perhaps a new beginning, not only for the narrator and the characters in the story but for the reader as well. Later in this book you will be given specific instructions for preparing the final draft of your story for submittal to editors, and the procedures required which will invite respectful attention from most editors.

2

GETTING STARTED

Who can become a selling writer? Everyone!

Everyone with a serious desire to write and perseverance in learning the proper rules, can sell at least *one* story—his or her own story.

"I've got all these stories bottled up inside me," one of my students told me, "but when I try to put them down on paper I just freeze up."

She is not alone in this experience.

Many well-established professional writers "freeze up" when starting a new story. Often they sit and stare at the typewriter for hours not sure where or how to begin. Some "sit it out" until inspiration flows; others break the jinx by using a tape recorder. Talking to it is a lot like talking to an invisible friend. Once started, the story unfolds without much effort and usually with more spontaneity and natural suspense than if you were pecking a typewriter.

This method was used to record a most fascinating story experienced during childhood by one of my neighbors. Sometimes we ran into each other at the market or filling station and took time to chat a while.

"I envy you people who can write," he confessed when I told him I'd sold another story. "I've always wanted to, but I don't know how and I haven't time now to go back to school to learn how it's done."

"Why do you want to write?" I asked.

"Well, I've got the damndest story bottled up inside me. I've 'lived' through it so many times for twenty years I can almost recite it but when I try to put it down it gets all twisted up."

He had whetted my curiosity. "Can you tell me what it's about?"

Presently, over coffee in the shopping center drugstore, he related a fantastic, almost eerie, true story about a ten year old boy in a small Tennessee town who, by accident, was forced to watch a young Negro girl give birth to a baby alone in the woods. He had almost cried out when he saw her sever the umbilical cord with her teeth, holding the newborn child in one hand, then wrap it in her sweater and fall back onto a bed of leaves, eyes closed. He thought she was dead. He was too frightened to run. He stayed behind a tree for a long time. He didn't know how long he stood there. Finally he saw her get up, take the child in her arms and, like an animal, scratch dead leaves and branches over the evidence of the birth on the ground. Then she walked slowly away. After a while the frightened boy gathered courage to run from what he had witnessed.

The boy went home. His mother was pregnant so he didn't want to tell her what he had seen. His father was working in the field of their small isolated farm. But the boy kept thinking of that lonely black girl, wondering where she had gone with her baby. He couldn't ask about it or her, so he tried to forget what he had seen.

When his mother's time came near, the boy's father arranged for her to go into the county hospital. But two weeks before her time, the mother fell on the back porch and brought on early labor. It was a Saturday morning and the father had gone into town for parts for the tractor, taking the three older children with him. They had no telephone. His mother needed help, but the boy couldn't leave her to go for the neighbor a mile down the road. The baby was already being born.

"You'll have to help me," the mother told him.

Terrified, the boy ran from room to room getting the things she told him to bring: newspapers for the bed, clean blankets, scissors. And to sterilize the scissors by holding them over the kitchen stove's gas flame. While he was doing this he heard his mother scream. Panicked, he ran from the kitchen, across the yard and into the woods, and he threw himself on the ground sobbing until he had no more tears.

"I cried because my mother was hurting and because I was scared. Then I saw I still had the scissors in my hand. I thought I could hear my mother calling to me for help, but I knew it couldn't be because the house was too far away. I remembered the black girl I'd watched that day and suddenly knew why my mother had asked for the scissors to be sterilized with heat. I ran as fast as I could back to the house."

His mother was lying there on the bed where he had left her, the baby between her legs. She called to him, "Cut it, Billy! Cut it or I'll die."

Somehow he got the courage to do what she asked while she gave directions. Afterward he cleaned things up the way she told him to. The baby was asleep in his mother's arms, wrapped in the clean blanket, when his father and the other children returned.

"The whole ordeal still haunts me. I don't know how I ever did what I did. It was like someone stood beside the bed guiding my hand, and keeping me from getting sick."

"God was helping you, Billy," I said, half expecting him to laugh.

Instead he looked at me a moment, then said, "You know, I think you're right. It couldn't have been otherwise. I remember my mother crying out afterward, 'Thank You, God, oh thank You!'"

After a while I said, "And all that happened over twenty years ago. Yet you had no trouble telling me about it, even in great detail. So why don't you rent a tape recorder, Billy, and tell the same story to it. Get someone to type it for you, then you can develop the scenes, using dialogue, giving it depth by telling how this brought you to a fuller awareness of God . . . ."

I made a few other suggestions about how to get started, story construction and scene placement.

"I'll do it!" he said. "Will you help me with it when I get it down on paper?"

It didn't need too much changing, only a little editing here and there. It was the first sale in a long succession of sales. The tape recorder had given him the impetus he needed to get his writing career started.

If you have a story to tell, but freeze up when you look at a tablet of paper or a typewriter, rent a tape recorder. It takes only a little practice to learn to use one. Pretend the microphone is a person, someone you know, someone you would confide in. Then just *talk*.

Most recorders come with a foot pedal for transcribing. A local high school typing student will transcribe your tape, for a nominal fee, into a first or "rough draft." Read this rough draft and make the changes you want to make. Cut out all the "rambling" which has no bearing on the story you are trying to tell, add additional bits of information about your characters which you may have left out or which will help the reader "know" them better. When you have completed the story to your satisfaction you will be ready for final typing. If you have a story "in progress" at the time you start reading this book, it would be advisable for you to hold up the final typing until you have finished reading the book. You may find important facts covered herein which will help you to improve your story and give it more reader impact. Then follow the detailed rules set forth later.

But if you're still "thinking about" the stories you intend to write someday when you get around to them, here are some basic rules which will help you get started:

Story Subject

The first step, of course, is to decide what particular problem in your life you want to write about. In making that decision, consider the overall dramatic elements of the story, then ask yourself how many hundreds—or thousands—of those reading the story would be interested in it or be able to identify with you throughout the experiences portrayed. If the subject does not have mass reader appeal, it is best to select another story.

Theme Sheet

This is the second step. A *theme sheet* may be short or very long. It is a method of writing notes to yourself about the characters in your story: what each character looks like, his or her temperament with particular attention to qualities that will make that character appeal to the reader the way you want him or her to appeal—sympathetic or otherwise; and special traits which make the character strong or weak, lovable or disliked, etc. Many professional writers prepare a "theme sheet" on each character in the story to make sure they fit the story's needs in their individual roles, and to avoid contradictions which can creep in later on. The main characters are, of course, most important. Novice writers often forget that the people in their stories are complete strangers to the editor or reader. Even the narrator herself, or himself. You must make them come alive, make the editor or reader see them as you *know* them. Presenting yourself, how you look and the kind of person you are, should be handled without making you seem conceited. Often this is achieved through dialogue or what others have said about you; that is, indirect narrative. Such as "Mother always said I was (pretty, bold, shy, plain, etc.)" However you want your characters to appear, *you* must know the details yourself before you start writing, then make the reader see them as you do.

Preparing Your Theme Sheet

In my own writing, I find the following general directions have worked well for me and have passed these along to students; either individual pupils or in class groups.

Put the title of the story at the top of the page. This can be a "working" or tentative title, but it should indicate what the story is about without telling the reader too much which might destroy suspense or interest. In other words, enough to intrigue but not give away the story, while also indicating the general theme, such as "I was an unwanted child . . .," or "I wanted to stay young forever." The theme of a story is what you intend to confess, and by means of the story prove or disprove the rightness or wrongness of what you did or what happened.

Next, decide what you want that proof to be, and put it down on your theme sheet.

Follow this with individual descriptions of your characters as mentioned earlier. These should include in this order:

1—Sex, age, and physical appearance.

2—Personality traits: jealousy, laziness, fears, selfishness, etc.

3—Attitude toward opposite sex, both as a youngster and at the time the story happened.

4—Education. This is for the purpose of determining the style of the character's dialogue, manner of speech, and mental comprehension. If, for instance, the character got no farther in school than the fifth grade, he or she wouldn't talk (or comprehend) the same as a high-school or college graduate.

5—Profession. Present job or office position. If it has changed from what the character wanted it to be or had trained for, indicate this. For instance, she had wanted to be a nurse but her parents sent her to business school to become a private secretary; and this fact—whatever the change or reason—could have a bearing on what happened to her.

6—Hobbies, if any. Also, character's attitude toward hobbies in general; believes they are good, or merely a waste of time.

7—Religious beliefs. If none, say so, and say *why*. Again this fact may motivate behavior in the story, influence him or her to becoming a cheat, a bigamist, a murderer, etc.

8—Social status. Modest circumstances with a simple way of life, or born to an affluent life with parental indulgences which may have brought on the problem being confessed. You indicate the social status by describing the kind of house, car, clothes, vacations, etc.

9—Parents' education, income, profession, religion. This information, which is termed background information, may play a large part in the reasons for the main character's problem, or misbehavior: such as childhood inhibitions, deep-rooted resentments or some other "hang-up."

10—Ambitions. The character's goal in life even if it is not the theme of your story. For instance, on your theme sheet you may have stated that Mary's ambition is to become a good wife and mother, but her problem may come about because she is working to help out with household expenses.

Story Development and General Outline

Once you have determined the theme and prepared the information about your characters you are ready to develop the story. The first thing to consider here are the *two opposing definable philosophies* the story must have. In other words, the two conflicting opinions regarding a solution to the problem. For example, should Mary leave Joe and their child, and marry the man she is now infatuated with and believes she loves, or renounce what she believes is a great and true love?

Your outline for developing the story should indicate which decision Mary will make. Next, decide the time element of the story: will it cover a day, a month, a year or longer? If a longer period is needed to tell the story, treat the earlier years in "flashback" segments.

Contemporary stories are most saleable. But the events which lead up to and contribute to the contemporary story may have great influence on why the story happened and how it is resolved in terms of problems, mistakes, regrets, etc. This is termed the "time arc" of your story. It can build suspense for the reader or make the events which compose the story more convincing and realistic. For example, suppose Joe has to be at a certain town by a certain date or miss out on: (the job he's worked toward for five years, or lose again the childhood sweetheart he has just found after several years)—or any number of "if's."

Be sure to cover the seasonal holidays in the story if the time element extends through the entire year, or more than one year.

Next, state where the story takes place, and supply details about the town or place. Much of this information should also be on your theme sheet but perhaps presented more briefly there. You now expand your outline to include more descriptions and unusual characteristics of the place. (A dying town, since the mine closed down; a village or small town where everyone knows everyone else's business, etc.) The important point is to make the reader see and feel the atmosphere of the place, so that he will also understand and sympathize with or condemn the main character's problem or misbehavior.

Writing Your Dialogue

The best definition I know for dialogue is "spoken emotional reaction." Think about that a minute. Isn't that largely what people talk about? And *why* they talk? In the kind of story you may be writing dialogue must be *the mirrored reflections of the main character's inner self.* On the other hand, dialogue which seems mere chitchat or idle discussion is often used to portray attitudes or characteristics of the speaker which have bearing on the story. This is termed *point of issue.* It ties in with the advice given above—two opposing philosophies or differences of opinion.

Keep this one point clearly in mind: All dialogue must progress your story, keep it moving ahead, whether that dialogue is direct conversation between two or more people, or giving the reader information about those people which is needed to understand what is about to happen or what may be threatening one of the main characters.

Dialogue must also be within the comprehension of the character speaking, or listening. For instance, a preacher would not use the "lingo" of a lumberjack, a bartender the manner of speech of a car salesman. You, the writer, may be any one of these—a lumberjack, salesman, etc., but unless *you* are speaking and the story is about you, you must give your main character his or her kind of natural speech, and this should reflect his education and way of life (lazy or ambitious). But be sure this is the same as you have set down on your theme sheet.

Here are a few basic "don'ts" about dialogue: Do not use dialogue for long-winded background explanations. Use narrative if it is necessary for a character to relate something to someone else in the story. Like this: Lead into the background narrative needed by a short exchange of dialogue, then switch to narrative—(He went on to tell me about . . . .)

Do not let your characters go into tirades to express anger, disgust, dismissal, etc. Most of the time one word, or two, will be sufficient. "No!" "Never!" "Get out!" "I hate you!"

Do not use a great deal of dialect. Instead, *indicate* the type of dialect the character may speak by using an occasional word: "you-all" or drawled words to show a Southern accent; or use a speaking manner to indicate some foreign accent which is typical of a particular country—French, German, Spanish.

Do select words which create an immediate image or emotional reaction; and words which have a beat or rhythm. "The eerie cry," "the train's lonely wail," "whispering leaves," etc. Often the way a sentence is punctuated changes its entire meaning or emphasis.

Dialogue *must always* express emotional intensity of one degree or another: strong, fearful, sad, joyous, anxious, etc.; reflect the inner emotion of the character, and frequently his or her *intended action* as well.

Avoid trite and overworked words and phrases such as "he hissed," "he snarled," "she barked," "she laughed"—one cannot speak and laugh at the same time. You may, however, use "he said, laughing" or "he said, frowning."

Avoid over-use of "uh" and "ah" to indicate stuttering or hesitancy; and *never* indicate laughter by the use of "hah! hah!" There may be times and places for stuttering and stammering in your story—such as a character with a speech impediment, or occasionally to express embarrassment or evasion of a question or situation. Learn to judge where such usage is effective and where it may bore or annoy the reader.

Keep in mind at all times the basic purpose of dialogue in a story: *to express inner thoughts, opinions, or wishes.* Otherwise let your characters act, indirectly showing—and often more forcefully—their feelings and desires.

3

GUIDE LINES AND EXAMPLES

Contemporary films, plays and novels have run the gamut of sex. Nudity is not only permissable on stage and screen but, to a high degree, on beaches, beside swimming pools private or public, and too frequently on public streets. Book writers seem to vie with one another in portraying actual sexual scenes in minute detail; scenes once confined to the *Police Gazette*, or backroom stag parties. The dime novel of earlier times, once the target of moralists, reads like a Sunday school picnic compared with many bestsellers today.

Editors of confession magazines do *not* want this kind of story.

Confession magazine readers do *not* want this kind of story.

Both editors and readers *do* want stories about ordinary people with everyday kinds of problems—the kind of problem or dilemma in which the reader himself (or herself) may be involved at the time.

Writers of confession stories therefore are not asked to compete with uncensored films and bestseller sex novels. What you write is presumably your own story. It is a personal-experience story. And whether that story deals with some basic sex problem or not, it can be presented with emotional impact without resorting to offensive language or descriptions.

Husbands and wives, facing home and family or money problems, are presumed to have satisfactory marital relationships. It is when their troubles bring about a change in this relationship that sex, to some degree, enters into a story dealing with the combined problems. The only four-letter word you ever need to use in your confession story is the word "love."

Let me illustrate this principle by excerpts from my story which was published in *Personal Romances*. It was titled "I Was Whistle Material." The idea for the story was derived from a conversation overheard in a hospital waiting room between a very attractive young woman and her friend. The attractive girl had just been told by her doctor that she must have one breast removed because of cancer.

I thought about this all the way home from the hospital where I had visited a friend recovering from minor surgery. Suppose, I asked myself, my friend had been given the news I had just heard? What would she have done, how would she have reacted? Would she have told me about it? Or would she have guarded her secret not only from close friends but from family, too? Suppose she had a husband? Piece by piece the story began to take shape in my mind. This is how it was finally developed:

In our bedroom Kerry said all of the nice things that make me feel so loved, so desired. And most of all, he said, was the pleasure of not having to make love on schedule. But all I could think was—early tomorrow is trash pick-up and I've got to find the Planned Parenthood calendar! I couldn't get a new one without Kerry knowing it, and I didn't remember my "safe" days that were marked on it. I got cold and sick inside, lying there trying to think while Kerry murmured and pulled me closer. When I mumbled I was tired, he only grew more tender.

"Let Doc Kerry make you feel better, sweetheart," he said. For answer I drew away, tried to ease out of his arms and oh, dear God, what an effort it was.

Aloud I begged, "Please, Kerry, not tonight. I'm sorry but I just don't feel—"

"Well, okay—" he stopped me. "Never let it be said I took my wife by force." Then, as if sorry for his words, he reached over and kissed my cheek. "That wasn't a nice thing to say, was it? I'm sorry. Guess you've had a big day at the office," he apologized. "And there's always tomorrow." We both settled down to sleep.

But I could tell by his breathing that Kerry lay awake, hurt and puzzled by my behavior. And I lay awake too, with a nervous anxiety to get up, to go out to the trash barrel. The trash truck usually came about six-thirty in the morning while Kerry was dressing, so I had to get it tonight. It seemed like forever before Kerry fell asleep and I knew it was safe to slip out of bed. It took ages to find the calendar, then I took it into the kitchen.

I was at the table trying to tape it together when Kerry appeared in the doorway, then came over to see what I was doing. There was a horrible moment that stretched into eternity before he spoke.

"So you didn't mean a word of it?" he declared. "You no more wanted a baby than the man in the moon, did you? You didn't intend to stop working now or ever. It's far more important that you buy all the fancy gadgets you want for the house than it is to be a mother." He said it all in such a flat, odd tone, I knew there was no use trying to deny or explain, then.

"I guess all this waiting," he went on, "all your promises, all your words about how you couldn't wait to get pregnant, how much you loved me—it was all just words! Maybe you're just in love with that body of yours—don't want to risk changing it. Well, you won't have to worry anymore."

"Kerry, I do love you! And I meant everything I said." I wanted him to put his arms around me, to hold me close, while I told him why we had to wait to have our baby. I wanted to tell him what the doctors wanted to do to me, but I couldn't get the horrible words out. So I sat there and he went on, calling from the hall. "Goodnight, Maura. I've got a big day tomorrow," and seconds later I heard the door of the spare room slam shut—the room that was to be our nursery.

The foregoing scenes present the cause of the problem and builds up to the crisis created by it. The balance of the story deals with how Maura learned to face her dilemma and what she did about it. Would she mature through this experience or run away from it? In a later section of this book I have used this story, broken down sentence by sentence, to explain techniques of scene development and placement, and the purpose each sentence served to make the story real and inspirational.

Sex situations in stories which once were considered shocking or taboo, today are absorbed in a more permissive approach to human behavior. Young people are exposed to more training on the subject in home and school. Sex education is a part of the cirriculum of many elementary and grade schools; as accepted as classes in reading, mathematics and grammar. Words and phrases which once were spoken in whispers behind closed doors have become a part of our everyday vocabulary. Rape. Sex offender. Venereal disease. Tragically, such things have become so common they are no longer *basic material* for a complete story. These are now used as *a situation which brings about the problem of the story.* The problem which you, the author, must solve through logical story-plot and other events contributing to the main character's dilemma.

During World War II, a popular problem or plot situation was one in which the office worker—female clerk, stenographer, receptionist, or private secretary—became the "other woman" in her boss' life, or of an officer stationed in the locality. Men were in short supply with most of the unattached in the armed services. This situation automatically created a "story situation." And to some degree it is a situation that still creates many problems for young women today. But if you use it, make sure you update it. Motivate it through today's environment and social customs. The "other woman" is as old as history and is likely to continue to be a part of civilized behavior. Because of this she will always provide good story material.

Most World War II or Korean War backgrounds are not suitable for today's "confession" stories because of different behavior patterns. Sex attitudes make it unnecessary for the young girl who finds herself pregnant to pretend she is a war widow to hide her child's illegitimacy. Today that girl is more likely to continue attending her school classes during pregnancy and later, take the child to school with her every day where it is cared for in a school nursery. Sexual relations without benefit of marriage are accepted by many, not as a "sin" but merely an inconvenience if a child is the result of the relationship.

However, these new attitudes also provide a great variety of dramatic situations suitable for magazine stories and books. The old formula went something like this: Betty lets her parents raise her illegitimate son as their own, promising never to claim the child. Out of this promise her "problem" develops when the boy is four years old. Betty falls in love with Robert who thinks all brides are virgins and certainly assumes Betty is. But a few weeks before the wedding her father dies. Betty now feels her child should have the security and love of a father as well as a mother and wants him to share her new life. But her mother is too attached to the child to let him go; contends she needs the boy more than ever now that she is alone. The arguments end up in the courts. *Betty is faced with a decision*: forfeit her right to the boy forever, or risk losing Robert by telling him Tommy is her son and not her little brother.

Or, take the same situation in reverse. Betty's mother insists she take her boy when she marries Robert. Her mother wants to be free from child-care responsibilities to pursue a life of her own. Again Betty is faced with a deci-

sion which is difficult. The writer must create a satisfactory solution without resorting to fate (acts of God
such as fatal accidents), miracles or coincidences. Whatever
the solution it should subtly contain an element of guid-
ance for young readers who might be faced with similar
problems. Betty must also *vindicate herself* through the
solution to her problem; mature mentally and emotionally
because of a deeper understanding of right and wrong,
wisdom or foolishness; learn to consider others—in this
case, what is best for her son rather than what will be the
least embarrassing to herself or Robert.

Let's try updating a similar situation in today's more
permissive society.

Betty's problem now is different but just as serious. Her
child has remained with her parents while she finished high
school, but is openly admitted to be her child. However
Robert, who does not expect Betty to be virginal (most of
the "chicks" he knows aren't), does *not* want another
man's child. Betty must decide whether to give up her son,
or Robert whom she loves passionately. Here again Betty,
in finding a solution to her problem, must *vindicate* herself, mentally and emotionally. And in this case the child's
welfare *has* to be her first concern. Will she relinquish
Robert, or give her child in adoption to a family that is
childless and can give him advantages neither she nor
Robert, or both together, could now provide? Many kinds
of solutions are possible here which a creative, imaginative
writer can handle in a variety of ways.

Even in today's freer society, there are grave problems
confronting youth which still are based on "sinful" or
imprudent behavior. But the problems are emotional now

rather than moral; that is, it is the emotional disturbance in most situations that the girl experiences which creates her problem, rather than a guilt complex.

For example: Sue and Ned are in high school and going steady, often spending weekends at a beach or mountain resort. They talk about getting married sometime, but there's no hurry. They're deeply in love and that is all that matters. Then Sue gets pregnant. Ned has a "thing" against marriage from necessity. He insists upon abortion. Sue believes that abortion is the same as committing murder; besides, she wants this child. It is *their* child! Ned wants to go on to college; he can't do that with a wife and child to support. His solution to the problem is to split.

Now Sue has to decide whether to have the child, quit school and get a job, and hope Ned will return to them when he "gets his head on straight"; or have the abortion which she believes is wrong and dangerous. Whatever her decision, it must vindicate Sue at the time or later on; that is, suppose she has the abortion and lives through it but the child dies. Remorse and mental suffering bring her to new awareness of responsibility and self-respect; to understand that everyone is responsible for his or her own actions, not through fear of scandal, but because the right way is the only way to keep self-respect.

Much the same story can be told from Ned's viewpoint with equally strong emotional and constructive values. Let's suppose Ned has a "hangup" against *having* to marry, and just splits with no apparent concern for what happens to Sue. He rationalizes his behavior, tells himself it was the smart thing to do to leave; how does he know the kid's his or someone else's. A year goes by. He has a good job but he's still "loving them and leaving them," although not entirely out of selfishness; simply that he can't forget Sue—or the child he now admits could not have been anyone's but his because he knew Sue was a one-man girl and wouldn't have played around with anyone else after they started going steady.

The problem he faces is whether to go back and find out what happened to both of them, or leave things as they are. Maybe Sue's married now and the guy thinks the kid is his. If he goes back he'll make a worse mess of things than he's already made. Whatever his decision, it must vindicate him in one of two ways: learn from the hard lesson he brought on himself out of fear and selfishness; or go back and find out what happened. If Sue is married and happy he will go his own way without revealing himself to them, but if she is still single, supporting their child, there could be a reconciliation, in which case both Sue and Ned have learned that love is not something to take for granted; that it must be earned as well as accepted.

One of my own stories which was published in *Tan* magazine used a similar problem theme and was titled "I Hope My Child Dies!" It was told from the girl's viewpoint showing the anguish and trouble she experienced when her high school sweetheart's mother discovered her son had made a girl pregnant and forced him to leave the town. But the boy did not know about the pregnancy. Later, when he learned about the baby, he defied his mother and returned to the hometown to marry the girl he still loved. The girl vindicated herself, however, before his return by risking her own life to save the life of her baby. The story had a happy ending.

Let's take a different kind of sex involvement. Herman is a young and rather attractive married man with an invalid wife. He tells himself he is "only human" and entitled to a normal life, and Francine is quite agreeable to taking care of his emotional needs. She has a good job, an apartment of her own, and doesn't want to get married. So what's the harm? They're not hurting anyone; what his wife doesn't know won't hurt her. Then, after a year or so, things begin to get "sticky." Francine falls in love with him and wants to make the relationship permanent. Herman is not in love with Francine, nor does he intend to divorce his invalid wife.

How is Herman to solve his problem? He has several possibilities which you, the writer, must select and develop to a convincing conclusion with some element of inspiration to others reading the story who may be in a similar situation. But because this is a rather "worn" problem theme—true or false, many restless husbands have used it to justify their own philandering—you must strive for a sincere and original solution. Do not depend upon the invalid wife's conveniently dying, or Francine being "swept off her feet" by a new love. Herman is the wrongdoer; he is the one who must vindicate his behavior. But he must do so with conviction for the reader and a realization of new values; or a reappraisal of old ones such as his marriage vows, and "do unto others."

"I love Bill, I really do," Elsie confides to her girlfriend during lunch hour in the cafeteria at Mayfield High, " . . . and I know he's going to get a good job after graduation, so I don't mind waiting for him. But he says I've got to prove I love him. You know . . . go all the way *now*. I'm scared, Lillie. I don't want to lose him to another girl! I just don't know what to do . . . ."

There are many others with this same problem. Girls with strong moral standards because their parents' teachings had not fallen on deaf ears. You, the writer, must decide what a girl in this situation would do or should do. You must show ultimately that the average well-brought-up young woman still has a sense of moral behavior, not because she is prudish, or "out of things," so to speak; but because she is aware of consequences that could easily destroy the love she feels for the young man in question.

For instance, Elsie might consider several evasive methods to hold the boy she loves but she would finally tell Bill that if he really loves her he will respect her wishes and wait until they can marry instead of "stealing" the rights of marriage in advance. However, in creating the solution to this story, don't take the easy way to let Elsie out of her dilemma, such as using her allowance for oral contraceptives or other preventative measures. To do so would be merely compounding her problem, not solving it.

For instance: if the confession being made in the story deals with how the narrator became pregnant by the young man she loved, it might be handled as follows:

> We slipped away from the others on the beach who were so busy cooking their hamburgers on the fire. They didn't notice us leave. "I've got to talk to you," Tom said, while he hurried me down the beach to the shelter of the huge rocks. But the second we both fell exhausted and laughing from our running in the loose deep sand, he took me in his arms and kissed me.
>
> "Oh Edie, Edie—I love you so!" he whispered against my throat and I said I loved him, too, more than anything in the world. Then he kissed me again

and I tried not to let the tears come to my eyes by thinking that this was the last night he would hold me in his arms for a long time—maybe never again.

He had eased me back onto the sand and put his sweater under my head and now he raised up on his arm and just looked at me and touched my mouth with his fingers. "Edie—you're the only girl in the world I'll ever want—you know that—and I want to marry you as soon as I get back and get a job. I'll be old enough then, but maybe I won't come back. Guys are getting killed over there every day."

"Don't say such things!" I cried, pulling his face down to mine again. "Oh, Tommy, if anything ever happened to you I would want to die too!" I said, and I meant it. Then, I don't know what came over me, but I couldn't get enough of his kisses. And when his hands began to fondle me and the trembling excitement I could feel in his body swept through mine, too, I didn't try to stop him like I had other nights. I wanted him as much as he wanted me. And all I could think was, at least we'll have this night—I'll always have this night to remember . . . .

Tommy had been gone three months and I had just gotten my first letter from him, the day I went to Doctor Ryan and learned I was pregnant.

From the analysis of the foregoing example you must have realized that this story is the *result* of sex, not the act of sex itself. It is the problem which developed *because* of sex, or lack of it; or sex with the wrong person or at the wrong time. In other words, sex is *assumed* by the reader; not depicted in graphic detail.

Keep in mind always that your story plot develops as your characters develop. This is a primary rule: Change must come about through your character's action, not because of coincidence or the interference of others.

Here are some reminders which should be reviewed each time you start a new story:

The Plot. This is a carefully planned scheme or series of actions, for or against, someone or some thing. All plots contain situations and episodes. In fact, all strong plots must use several situations and episodes to develop the story you want to tell. For instance, you may get story *ideas* from situations and people encountered in your daily life, but these do not make the complete story. A complete story must have a beginning, a middle, and an end. In other words: a reason for being, the effect of situations and events in the course of the story upon your characters, and the solution to the problem such situations and events have created. As in life, story characters must mature in some way through situations and episodes you have created for them in the plotting of your story; and find solutions within themselves or by means of greater wisdom or understanding gained through the problems experienced.

Plot Development. Always begin a story with an exciting or interest-getting situation. Suspense, sudden tragedy, a moment of stark terror; something so electric that the reader will want to go on reading, find out what happened and why.

A good plot development makes use of the unexpected, surprises; is never predictable by the reader. It is based on the principle that "nature is always working against the best laid plans of your character." So keep the reader guessing and at the same time, concerned. This is achieved by two basic areas: *conception* and *projection.*

Conception covers the factors the writer is concerned with in deciding how his main character is going to change, in the course of the story, his present way of thinking. This is your "theme meaning," and it must be a definable one; a meaning that burns within him. For instance, in my story "I Was Afraid of Sex," the definable theme was: lack of proper knowledge about sex creates fear and frustration in a child toward sex in later life. The theme of a story may be one of vague abstraction, but this meaning must have a direct application to some area of everyday life. A psychological timeliness. The application of meaning which is universally accepted or recognized.

Projection. This area covers the visible allegory of your meaning. The writer must supply himself with various elements such as character, motive, goals or opposition; the carrying lines of conflict; and the backdrop of struggle. These should be introduced no later than the second scene of your story. The main plot also should include the promise of future drama involving these elements, and always as seen through the eyes of your main character or as portrayed in his thoughts. Each element must be introduced in cross-relationship with another element, never in agreement with it. It is this main line of conflict within your main character which holds the plot together. Keep this in mind for it is the *supporting beam* of every story. It is created by the burning dedication of one central character to achieve a specifically defined *goal.*

The climax of your plot occurs when this main line of conflict within the main character is faced, solved, the goal reached—or abandoned.

Any convincing story also needs its *secondary lines of conflict*. These give dimension to the story and permit the introduction of opposing philosophies in a variety of areas—religion, accepted customs, or opinion on what may be considered "good" or "bad." Again using "I Was Afraid of Sex" to illustrate the point: Here the secondary line of conflict concerned the mother's earlier life and her own sex hangup, which was resolved along with the son's later on-stage problem.

Backdrop Line. This is in addition to your main line and secondary line, and is used to strengthen your plot. It is concerned with the same philosophical clash and is expressed in mass terms—humanity above and beyond the awareness or control of your main characters. It must reach a conclusion both thematically and philosophically along with the solution to the on-stage problem of your main character. For instance, the theme and philosophy of the backdrop line in "I Was Afraid of Sex" is projected through the dialogue of the prostitute the husband sought to "prove" his manhood.

Time Element. This is a vital element in all plotting. It is the time factor, the "time arc" mentioned earlier, which is moving against the central character while trying to achieve his goal. In "I Was Afraid of Sex," this element was used in the sequence of the mother's absence while visiting a daughter in another state, which gave the husband time to find himself—to see things differently, more maturely, and to solve his own problem. The fact that the main character of a story is always working against some time element creates suspense for the reader and urgency for the story character. And these contribute to the impact of your story since all of us, to one degree or another, are constantly working against the pressure of time.

General rules are necessary to the teaching of writing. However, I have found that once the student has been informed on these main rules, they are better focused for him by means of reproducing an illustrative segment of a story, or the entire story as published.

4

SEX THEMES WITHOUT OBSCENITY

At what age is sex no longer important to readers, or as a necessary ingredient for interesting and saleable stories?

The answer depends to some extent upon the magazine you expect to sell to. In the confession story market, sex is a vital element. It is almost invariably both the motivation for the story and the basis of its conclusion. And it plays an important role in the resolution of the problem confronting your main character or characters.

Thanks to modern medicine and a more universal knowledge of nutritional diets, age (in terms of the number of one's years) no longer limits most people's interest in or enjoyment of sexual relationships. In some cases men and women have reported increased fulfillment in such relations during their middle and late years. Often, too, such relationships become more meaningful during a second or even third marriage. This, basically, is the psychology behind most "illicit" or "cheating" relationships. Changing mates adds adventure and excitement.

Today's woman who takes pride in her appearance is admired by the opposite sex at any age from sixteen to seventy, and for many has the allure she had at a much younger age. Taking pride in one's appearance means keeping your figure, using makeup artfully, and selecting your clothes with good taste rather than merely "following the fashion." Nothing is less attractive than a mature woman who tries to recreate youth or attract attention of male suitors by means of frilly clothes and too much makeup. Older women whose grooming and dress are in keeping with their maturity are far more likely to find devoted admirers.

The same general rule applies to men. A man who is slovenly about his grooming, or merely careless about shaving regularly and having his hair cut properly, is not likely to get many second glances from pretty girls or desirable woman. Today's mature man is, however, more aware that "clothes make the man" and of the allure of "smelling good." On the contrary, today's youth—male and female —is inclined to be less concerned with good grooming; rather, they trend toward the so-called natural look which somehow still has not changed the age-old law of attraction between the sexes in a more permissive society.

These are points worth remembering when planning or plotting a story, whether for a confession magazine or one of the more general magazines. Understanding the psychology of human beings of all ages, male or female, will make a story more believable; will allow the reader to live the story with the characters and benefit from their experiences.

Confession magazines, however, normally prefer stories about young people; young married or early middle-aged couples whose problems derive from the fact of having been together long enough to start taking one another for granted, becoming less attentive, less thoughtful. For instance, my story "She Wanted to Stay Young Forever" used some of these elements. If a story is mainly concerned with children who are able to get a new stepfather, make the children quite young so the mother can be fairly young too. Obviously, the story problem which you select will determine the ages of your main characters and how you develop the story. It is a good general rule to keep your main characters between twenty-five and thirty. Use teenagers or characters under twenty-five for premarital sex problems. Most things which are crises at age seventeen or eighteen would be taken in stride at age thirty or older. But because youth's problems are so seemingly insurmountable, confession or personal problems magazines want their stories. Stories of sacrifice, love's awakening, or loss of the beloved one through various reasons; stories of passion, selfish or unselfish indulgence, or the effects of these upon other lives.

Suppose, for example, the story you decide to write is based on a sex "hangup." Obviously your characters must be of an age when this particular problem would be crucial or at least of great importance. My story, "I Was Afraid of Sex," published in *True Experiences*, was developed from that theme when Edna, a neighbor, told me that her husband was "no good as a husband" because of the ideas about sex his mother had instilled in him when a child; that they had had sexual relationships only four times since their marriage—on their wedding night and three other times after long intervals of abstinence when she had become pregnant. But regardless of the truth of Edna's experience, I realized that no editor or reader would believe she had remained with her husband for more than five years under such circumstances. In real life, Edna finally got a divorce when she realized that her husband would never rid himself of his belief that sex was "nasty, sinful," and later remarried. But that did not make a plot for a story. So, what *would* make it a story? The *problem* each faced in their marriage, and how they *solved* it. Not by running away from it, but through understanding and caring enough for each other and their children.

The wife's problem was frustration and unfilled marital love. The husband's problem was his attitude toward normal sexual relationships. The story lay in *why* he had that attitude which made him unable to perform as a husband.

I wrote the story from the husband's viewpoint, and let him go back, in flashback, to his childhood, his teenage years, when his mother's influence was strongest. He was the character in the story who had created the problem of their marriage, therefore he was the one who must solve it. In plotting the story I decided to let its development prove that had the husband been taught as a child that the true meaning of sex in marriage was love and the bearing of children, he would not have created the problem which now threatened to wreck his marriage. Once he recognized what the problem was and why it existed, he could take the right steps to save his marriage and recapture his wife's love, like this:

I held Elsie tighter in my arms and I kissed her again. I just couldn't get enough of her now that I knew what her sweet soft mouth felt like. I could feel her breasts against my chest and then she was saying against my cheek that yes, she loved me too and would marry me. I was in such a fog or trance I didn't realize I had even asked her until she said that.

"Let's elope, Bill." Her voice was an excited little whisper, then she looked toward her house with the lights all on. "The folks won't mind. I know they won't. Weddings are so expensive and poor Papa has all he can do to feed the brood. Do *you* want to elope?" And on impulse I said, sure, that's what I wanted to do. It was up to her.

"Tomorrow! Let's do it tomorrow!" she said. "That way we will have the weekend and be back to work Monday." And in those next few minutes all of the plans were made . . . to pick her up at six in the morning and drive over to the JP in Greene County, then on to the motel in Clarksburg.

"We'd better call ahead for a reservation after the ceremony," she went on. Then she sort of laughed, a thin, embarrassed type of laugh. "I'd hate to spend my wedding night in a car! Making love on the back seat isn't for old married folks, is it?" and she snuggled closer to me.

But that second, I froze up inside because suddenly another night in the back seat of a car, Clyde Adams' old sedan, screamed through my head.

". . . And, Bill," she hesitated a second, "we haven't

had time to talk about things like where we'll live, or about sex . . . but . . . I don't want to get pregnant right away . . . I want to work awhile and save the money to buy a house and everything. So let's be, you know—careful—until I can go to a doctor and get a prescription for the pill."

Just then her kid brother came out on the porch and yelled, "Hey, Elsie! You guys got to quit necking now. Pop said to come on in; he wants to turn out the lights and stuff." And Elsie gave me a quick kiss. "I love you so much, Bill," she said. "I'm so excited I doubt I'll be able to sleep! I'll be on the corner at six, so they don't hear the car stop." Then she got out of the car and ran up her front steps and I drove home.

These next three paragraphs clearly define the problem that is to be solved—clearly state the *theme*; i.e., *is Bill going to ever be able to perform as a real husband?*

But I didn't go to bed. I was too sick. Elsie's words went around and around in my head. *We hadn't had time to talk about sex.* Even if we'd had the time I couldn't talk about it, because the only thing I really knew about sex was what I'd been taught by my mother, that *it was a dirty word.*

I didn't know how to make love to a girl. The only time I tried was that night in Tom Adams' car. What if my wedding night turned out like that night?

I paced through the house. I went to the phone to call Elsie to tell her I'd changed my mind; that I didn't want to get married. But I didn't dial the number. I didn't have the courage to talk to her. Because I couldn't tell her the reason. I couldn't tell her that I was afraid I couldn't be a real husband! That I had chickened out with Rosie from Denton; that maybe I still had the same "hangup" I had then—a hangup that started when I was just a little kid.

So much for the opening, the problem, the "setup." Next comes the first flashback, when Bill is about six years old. This flashback also tells the reader what the reader *should* know—no more, no less; i.e., family income status, religious beliefs, and the nucleus of this young man's frustration that later in life becomes his "problem." The "flashback scene" goes like this:

My father was a coal miner and he died with "black lung" when I was four years old. My mother got a job as housekeeper for the Dawsons. Mr. Dawson was the general manager of the mine and they were the most well-off family in the community. Those first two years my mother took me across town with her every day on the bus and I played in the Dawson's yard with their caretaker's two small children. Then I was old enough for the first grade.

The schools in Needle Hill were like everything else in town—grim-looking, delapidated, covered with a black dust that clung to all the buildings, with a drinking trough at the front door and outside toilets not too far from the back door.

This one afternoon—it was a warm April day—I didn't want to go back inside after recess. I still couldn't adjust to being indoors all day. So I hid behind the boys' outhouse until everyone had gone inside. I was watching a big fat yellow bee flutter around a dandelion near my feet and I wasn't aware of the girl until she spoke to me.

"Hiya," she said, coming close. "What you looking at?" I told her I was watching a bee. I talked quiet, like she was talking, for fear we'd be heard from the schoolhouse. She squatted down in the grass to get a better look at the bee, and I got down beside her. She was a big girl, about ten, with long stringy hair that kept blowing around. I don't know what was said or who said it, but before I knew what was happening she was unfastening my belt. "Y'all show me yours and I'll show you mine," she said. Then she pulled up her dress and I saw she wore nothing under it.

That was the second I looked up to find Mrs. Allen, the principal, staring first at my unzipped jeans, then over at the girl who was trying to pull her dress down fast. We were both taken into her office and made to stand in opposite corners. I knew by Mrs. Allen's attitude, and the few words she spoke, that something disastrous must have happened, but I had no idea what. I was six-and-a-half years old, and to me the difference between boys and girls meant wearing dresses or jeans, playing with dolls or tin cars from the ten cent store. But from that day on, *I knew the Devil himself was male*!

My mother was called to the school for a "conference" the next day. And that afternoon when I got home she was waiting for me.

She took me into the bedroom and gave me a beating with one of my father's old work shoes she'd taken out of the closet. She hit me so hard that after the first minute I was numb. The more she struck me the angrier she seemed to get, and her words came out in almost gasps. She said things I didn't understand then, about seeing I didn't grow up to be a selfish sex crazy son of the devil.

She finally wore herself out and threw the shoe across the room. I clung to the bedpost, too dazed and scared to move. When she got her breath she threatened me with all sorts of horrible things that would happen if I ever so much as "touched" myself—that it was dirty, nasty, sinful to do to a girl what I was doing when I was "caught" by Mrs. Allen. It didn't matter to anyone, I guess, that I hadn't done anything, and I didn't know then *what* I was supposed to have done. She went on about how "that thing" was on me for only one reason: to get rid of the poisons in my body. But the way she said it made me ashamed to even go to the bathroom for months afterward. And I was a big kid before I got over undressing only in the dark for fear someone might be peering in the windows to see that shameful part of my body.

Going to church to hear all about the hell waiting for the wicked was the only break in the motonony of living in Needle Hill. I had already heard it many times before I was six-and-a-half, but from that time on I would sit there on that hard wood bench and think the preacher was talking directly to me.

Next is about 350 words of informative narrative, showing the reader Bill's attitude toward girls and toward his mother; to bring him up to age seventeen when he asks Clyde Adams to arrange a double date for him with Clyde's cousin Rosie from Denton because he has read "sex" paperbacks and wants to really learn about sex. Then comes the scene with Rosie, the second "flashback":

We went out to the Red Eye, a place down the pike where you could get hamburgers and dance to the juke box. It was against the law, but kids could buy beer and wine and Clyde ordered some wine and a bucket of crushed ice for all of us. Rosie drank the wine like it was water. I didn't want to look like a cornball so I drank a small glass too. And after that I got the nerve to dance with Rosie when she asked me. Her skirt was so short sometimes the lace on her panties showed when she did a wiggle or a twist. Like Clyde had said, she was really built and her breasts bounced every time she did. I was just getting over being so shy and uncomfortable-feeling when Clyde said we were leaving. "How's about going to the Landing and look at the moon? Unless you know of a better place to go, Bill?" I said, no, the Landing was okay by me.

As though the Landing had some magic to its name, Marylou got closer to Clyde if that was possible, and Rosie pressed herself so close to me I could feel the pulse in her warm body with every breath she took.

"I'm cold, Billy boy," she said and I put my arm around her like I'd been wanting to do every since we got in the car. "You're groovy," she purred against me. "I wish there were more guys like you at that dumb school I go to. They're all runts. You think I got a nice shape?"

"Yes, you've got a beautiful shape." I got the words out, but that was all I could say. From the way Clyde knew just where to park his car beneath the huge old water oak trees with their veils of moss that hung almost to the ground in some places, I knew he and Marylou had come here often. He shut off the engine then opened the door for Marylou.

"I'll give you guys the car," he said. "We'll use the boat house—there's a cot in there." And just enough light came from the pole on the dock so I could see his grin and the wink he gave us. Then he and Marylou started up for the old frame building.

They hadn't disappeared from sight before Rosie was in my lap. The effects of the wine had worn off, but I couldn't think. I didn't want to think. I just did what she guided me to do. She put my hand on her breast and in the next second I was kissing her, and my hands were all over her. This was the first time I'd ever had the chance to feel a girl's flesh. She kept whispering things against my face and letting me know every way possible what she wanted me to do—exactly what I was on the verge of doing.

Suddenly all the night noises screamed into the car: the wind in the tree moss, the croak of a frog, the soft slap of the river against the wooden pailing—all became a thunderous roar in my ears, and the water came out all over my face and neck. I felt stifled, like I was going to choke. I shoved Rosie off me, all my passion and desire for her gone.

I reached over and yanked open the car door and practically fell out. By the time I got to my feet, she was there beside me. I was shaking, not from the cold April wind that came across the river, but because *I was scared! I was scared of sex—and my mother!* All I could think was *Mom would kill me!*

"What's the matter, Billy? Didn't you *want* to?" Rosie had both her hands hooked through my arm while she shivered against me. "Don't you like me? I thought you *liked* me."

"It isn't that." I took deep gulps of the cold air while I found the words. "It's just . . . well, it's not right. I'll probably not ever see you again . . . we only just met." I said the words as they came out. Then she put her head against my arm.

"Oh, Billy, that's the most beautiful thing in the world!" she said. "A boy's never said anything like that to me before. They always just want to make out. Girls expect it." I had started walking down to the dock. My hands were in my pockets. I didn't say anything more. I couldn't. Because she kept carrying on about what a *gentleman* I was, so *mature*, to be able to control my *passion*—how different from all the creeps she knew in her school in Denton.

"I don't really believe in giving in the first date, either, Billy," she said. "It's more fun to . . . you know . . . sort of fool around but not do anything the first date. Tomorrow we'll make Clyde and Marylou use the car and *we'll* take the boat house, okay? It's only fair we get the boat house tomorrow." And just then we heard the car horn toot and Clyde call out "Hey, you guys, come on. We better get going."

To this day I don't know what was said or done on the ride back to town, because all I could hear screaming through my head were things my mother had beaten into me about sin and lust and the devil. I was so relieved when we pulled up to my house and it was dark I could have cried, because, although I was seventeen, I was afraid to face my mother, to have her see the guilt and shame I was sure would show in my face.

It wasn't a lie the next day when I told Clyde I was sick and couldn't double date with him again. I really was sick. Mr. Dawson sent me home at noon because I had a fever, and I had the flu for the following week.

This ends the second flashback, which further developed the theme that Bill was terrified of sex, which resulted in his running out on his plan to elope with Elsie. I follow this with about 200 words of narrative which will tell about his shying away from girls, and emphasize his attitude toward his mother. I conclude with:

If Mom heard any of the wild stories about me from mothers at church, she didn't let on. But sometimes I'd see that her eyes were red and those nights she didn't eat much supper. Then when it was time for me to go to bed, I'd lay there in the dark feeling a bit sick to my stomach and take a long time to go to sleep. But because I had this "thing" about wanting to hurt her, I built a wall between us and before long we were almost strangers.

About 400 words of narrative here tell of his mother going to Raleigh to visit the sick aunt and about meeting Elsie. The groundwork is laid for the later change in attitude toward his mother through a scene where Bill is having supper with Elsie and her family which concludes:

And suddenly I knew what was so different here. A good feeling of love and warmth seemed to seep out from the walls to embrace them all; love and respect of the children for their mother and father showed in everything they said.

And that minute, a guilty feeling swept over me, thinking of how it was at home with me and Mom, how I treated my mother.

More narrative follows (about 250 words), telling of Bill's mother's notes which he ignores, and of his falling in love with Elsie. Now the story comes back on-stage to the opening, where Bill is faced with his problem:

I couldn't stop kissing her, and she didn't try to make me stop. When at last we were both exhausted, I cradled her head against my face. "I love you, Elsie. I love you so much," I said. "I've only known you a month and yet I can't remember not having known you." And those minutes I was completely free of my inhibitions I'd had about girls.

But now, watching the hands on Mom's old china clock racing around toward morning, it all screamed through my head again and I could feel the sweat come out on my face and on the backs of my hands, and I knew *I couldn't go through with it—I couldn't marry Elsie!*

The narrative follows to show him in his car, driving on the highway, stopping for gas, thinking of Rosie and Denton. He stops in a bar, has a double shot, and the story continues:

When I heard the word "Denton" I knew what had been in the back of my mind when I left home . . . .

I asked the bartender where I could find a girl. I had to prove to myself I was a man. His directions didn't take me too far from the truck stop, so I left my car there and walked, or rather, staggered. It was an old frame house set back in an overgrown yard. At three in the morning the lights were all on and there was music coming from a juke box. I was in such a fog I don't remember knocking or ringing a bell or anything until there I was, up in a sleazy looking bedroom with this gal who was handing me a highball.

"Don't get many young ones coming in here," she said, looking me over. "And when they do it isn't just for the fun and games like the oldsters . . . it's because they got problems. What's your hangup, Junior?" She took a deep breath and let out a sigh. "I'm bushed. This has really been a hard day's night."

I just looked at her. She was twice as old as I was, and her makeup didn't cover the drooping lines at her mouth or the crows feet at her eyes. All she had on was a bra and a pair of pants. A roll of flesh laid at her waist and her breasts were huge and flabby looking.

"Come on, Junior, drink up! Relax—tell Katie what's bugging you. I got certain cures for certain problems. You got a girl?" And I said, yes, I had a girl, and yes, I loved her. Then she went over and sat on the edge of the bed and took a couple of swallows from her glass before she went on. "Mama trouble? Afraid your girl will find out you're still a virgin? Or problem number three—your girl insists on walking down the aisle a virgin?"

Now it was my turn to drink. I needed it! I drained the glass, hoping the liquid would put out the fever raging inside of me. I fell into the only chair in the room when she said that's where I could put my clothes when I was ready. She kept talking while she went over to the beaten up old dresser and fixed herself another drink.

"You sure ain't talkative. You're really uptight. You young kids make me a little maudlin." For a second I thought she was going into a crying jag, the way her face twisted, but she didn't. ". . . because you don't *love* me. Now the old guys *all* love me. They come see me because they really *want* me. But you kids can't put love and sex together. You got to keep 'em separate. You got to really grow up before you learn the one needs the other." Then she reached for the Big Ben alarm clock and started to wind it. "You look kinda woozy. In case you go to sleep, what time you got to get up to go home?" she said without looking at me. "Go on, honey, get your duds off." Then she went back to the bed and sprawled out on it.

Like someone pushing my legs to make me walk, I went over and put my glass on the dresser top, then I stood there looking down at her and I thought I was going to vomit. She was repulsive-looking to me. And that second, all I could think of was Elsie's soft warm body, how wonderful it felt up against mine. I could almost feel her young firm breasts against my shirt, and echoing around in the room were the woman's words: ''You kids can't put sex and love together . . . you got to grow up before you learn the one needs the other."

Well, I grew up pretty damn fast. While I looked down at this Katie's work-worn flesh, I knew that for me sex and love *did* go together. I loved Elsie, *and she*

was the one I wanted to learn about sex from! She was
the one who could rid me of any hangups I had.

I made it to the door and out the hall and down
those steps so fast I was out on the porch again before
I heard her yell, "Hey, kid, come back here!" above
the sound of the juke box in the old parlor. But I kept
running until I got to my car.

The narrative which follows gets Bill back to his house and
sets the stage for the "obligatory scene," the "thematic
conclusion" of the story:

I went out to the kitchen to put on a pot of coffee,
and my eyes fell on Mom's apron hanging on the hook
by the stove. I had a sudden strangely overwhelming
urge to talk to her, to say I missed her—a fact I only
that second would admit to myself—and I wanted to
tell her about Elsie.

I didn't know my aunt's last name or address. I had
thrown away the cards Mom sent. So I went into my
mother's dresser where she always put things to find
the telegram that had taken her to Raleigh, sure that
she had saved it. It was there, alongside paid utility
bills and other papers. And to the back of the drawer
was a small packet of papers with a blue ribbon tied
around it. I never thought of my mother as a senti-
mental person. I lifted the packet out and looked at it
and realized I didn't even know my mother as a
person.

I knew it was wrong, but I untied the old ribbon to
see what was there. And those next few minutes I felt
like I was probing in a grave, the grave that had swall-

owed my mother's heart. There was my birth certifi-
cate and her marriage license with the JP's signature,
dated five months before my birth. There was a letter,
too, but it wasn't a love letter. Instead it was filled
with words that had to be read only once to be remembered forever. It was from my father, a man I scarcely
remembered: "... so you're pregnant and I'm to
blame," it said, "and your old man has thrown you
out. Well, it wasn't all my fault, you know, and I
didn't say anything that night about being in love or
getting married, and I didn't *run out* on you as you put
it. You knew I was thinking about coming here. I left
Raleigh and came here because Needle Hill was the
only mine hiring and I needed a job. Now you got
three choices: use this money for an abortion—ask
around at school; somebody's sure to know a doc—or
use the money for medical expense then put the kid up
for adoption and get yourself a job; or you can get on
the bus and come here and I'll marry you. Just remember it won't be like you got it at home." There was
more, but I couldn't read it.

She'd had three choices—and *I* was the one she
took ... and I had bombed out. Oh, Mama, I'm so
sorry! was all I could think. *I'm so sorry for all the
things I didn't do, and those I did.* My eyes stung with
tears and I had trouble seeing while I tied up the
bundle again. Sure, she had a "hangup" all her own,
but I could have made it easier for her to bear. And the
tears were for knowing now, too late, that I could have
eased some of the secret pain my mother knew all
those lonely loveless years, but I hadn't. Now dozens
of things spun around in my head—her obsession and

ignorance, perhaps, about sex when I was a little kid—
realizing the only way she knew to make sure I didn't
grow up and do something like my father had done
was to beat the fear of hell into me.

I took the telegram with my aunt's address out to
the phone and put the call through to Raleigh. My
mother answered. "Mom, how are things going?" I
asked her, and when she got over her surprise at hearing me and asking if anything was wrong, what did I
call for, I couldn't think of any words to say. You
can't break down a wall of years in a matter of
seconds. Besides, a thickness had come into my throat,
thinking of all the things I could have said on birth-
days, Mother's days. "Mom, I love you, and I've missed
you—a lot." I got the words out, but she didn't say
anything. And I could tell she was crying. I didn't want
her to cry—not any more. Then I was telling her about
Elsie, and I said I was going to get married.

She asked me when, and I looked over at the clock,
figuring it would take an hour to drive to Greene
County, but on impulse I said, "Mom, you want to see
me get married?"

"Only if you are in love," she said, and I knew from
her tone what it meant to her to say that. I assured her
I was, adding, ". . . and Mom, I'll try to make a better
husband than I did a son," and before I hung up the
receiver I had promised that we would drive over to
Raleigh and pick her up and take her with us to get
married.

Then I rushed around showering and shaving, and
those minutes were a nightmare, worrying about what
Elsie would do or say when she saw me.

It was a little after eight when I got to the Jackson's and I knew the whole family would be up and having breakfast. I didn't even knock. I just pushed open the door and rushed out to the kitchen. Elsie was at the table, all dressed, but her eyes were red and swollen, and seeing them was like having another knife stuck in me.

By this time I couldn't think or plan or try to explain. I just grabbed her arm and pulled her to her feet, then I looked at her father and mother who were both sitting with their mouths open and glaring at me. "We're eloping," was all I said, then I practically dragged her out the front door and to my car.

I hadn't said anything to her, neither did she talk to me, but as soon as I got in the car beside her I took her in my arms and I kissed her—and she kissed me back just as hard. That was all I needed to get on our way. She didn't ask any questions, she just snuggled up to me and kept her head on my shoulder.

But long before we hit the intersection to Raleigh, I said, "Elsie, I'm sorry if I hurt you. All I can say is I was scared, but I'm not anymore."

And that's all I had to say to her. But that night, after we had taken my mother back to her sister's house and we all had a glass of wine to celebrate, and we made plans for us to live together soon as Mom got back to Needle Hill, we drove out to the Wander Inn Motel for our two-day honeymoon. And I proved to Elsie and to myself I had nothing to be afraid of, ever again, and that when *sex* is coupled with *love* it is a beautiful word—and no "hangups" go with it.

Thus the problem was solved and what I intended to prove was proved. Bill would now be a "real" husband to Elsie.

5

MALE VIEWPOINT STORIES

Stories told from the male viewpoint are always in demand. And there is no one better qualified to tell a story from a man's viewpoint than a man. But as a rule, men do not get as involved with life's personal problems as women. A man is more likely to be concerned with material success or failure. He is more aware of actions than emotions. So, women quite often have to write much-needed stories from the male viewpoint. To do so, however, a woman writer must take the time to listen and to observe men's attitudes and behavior. She must understand their minds and emotions; try to think and talk in the story as a man would, and be direct, get to the point as quickly as possible.

Do not overact or become overly emotional in scenes. Be realistic in your approach to a problem, as a man would be. Most he-men are not dreamers who wait around for miracles to happen! Nor do they have the "Pollyanna" philosophy that everything will be fine tomorrow. Usually a man sees the problem and tackles it. They are likely to use one word instead of three if one word will say what they mean. Keep all of this in mind when writing the stories from the male viewpoint, and pay special attention to these points in dialogue.

No implication is intended that men are unemotional, or impervious to tears and heartache. On the contrary. But most men do *not* sit and suffer in silence when they are hurt by someone's actions or words. Someone else's confusing attitude does not keep them in doubt very long. Normally, a confrontation or direct questioning is used to "clear the air." The average man does not like uncertainty. In a male viewpoint story, see that the man recognizes his problem fairly early and decides to do something about it.

In writing your story you may awaken husbands to consider causes before they indulge in complaints about their wives; and ailing wives will bless you for it! At the same time, a housewife who has allowed herself to fall into slovenly ways may be brought to correct her shortcomings; or one who, as with Carrie, was always tired and gaining weight may be encouraged or inspired to do something about these things before her husband starts "looking around."

Many problems in the home which are a part of average everyday life can be used as basic story material. In fact, such situations make the most convincing stories because they deal with universal problems and therefore have wide reader-identification. First know *why* your characters behave as they do, then work out the best and most logical solution to their problem without resorting to impossible devices or too-easy answers.

To illustrate the importance of this basic premise, let's analyze a story published in *True Romances* which was titled "She Wanted to Stay Young Forever."

I wrote the story from the husband's viewpoint. I used as the *story-subject* (which is not the *problem*), an ingredient that seldom had been used up to that time in magazine stories; namely, menopause. The problem of the story was created when an attractive woman at thirty-five marries a man eight years younger than herself. After a while she starts worrying that he will do as her father had done with her mother: run out on her when she reaches menopause. Worry soon so overwhelms her that to cope with it she starts drinking, and by the time their daughter Karen is nine years old, the mother is a complete alcoholic.

Aware that love, patience and understanding on the part of those hurt by the "sinner" must always be the means of bringing the story to a satisfactory conclusion, I let the husband decide against divorce as a solution to the problem of an alcoholic wife. But gradually he ran out of patience with her and started condemning her weakness. Vindication came through ultimately realizing that his wife needed help, not criticism. He "matured," "grew up mentally," "came to realize."

Here is the way I handled the story:

I think the trouble began the day I brought my wife and new baby home from the pediatrician's first examination. I laid little Karen in her crib, fetched the satchel of baby bottles and spares from the car and took them to our room. Ethel was standing in front of the full-length mirror, studying herself from all angles. I stepped up behind her and buried my face in her abundant hair.

"That's quite a good-looking gal in the mirror," I said, meeting her glance before I kissed her on the back of the neck. "And I understand she recently had a youngster."

Ethel squirmed out of my arms and turned to face me. "Bill, do I look any different because I had a baby?" she asked in a more serious tone than I'd ever heard her use. "Do I look—older? Tell me, I want to know the truth."

I had a flip answer ready, but changed it quick when I saw Ethel's eyes. I held her tight to me, and although I meant every word I said, I exaggerated just a bit, knowing it would make her feel good. "Honey, I've never known a woman as exciting and beautiful as you are," I said, kissing her between words. "I've always had a feeling you had some secret connection with the Fountain of Youth in St. Augustine!"

"Now you're teasing me!" she said, hugging me tight around the neck. "But I love you for saying it!"

Just then a little squeal came from baby Karen, and Ethel went to check it. My eyes followed the quick, graceful movements of her slender form out of the room, and I honestly thought motherhood had made my wife more beautiful, if anything. And my love couldn't possibly have been greater.

Note that this opening sets Bill up as a pretty nice guy and the reader is pulling for him, wanting everything to work out right for him. But to justify his being the kind of man he was, a flashback scene is needed here. I used narrative to let the reader know how Bill had learned Ethel's age, and what his true attitude was about it. Like this:

I was secretly determined to make her forget the difference in our ages.

And I stuck to that resolve when, two months after our marriage, papers came from her insurance agent for me to sign. Ethel had apparently forgotten that her birth date was on one of the inside pages. I didn't tell her, because it added three years to the thirty-two she'd told me she was. If she was that self-conscious about her age, I had no intention of embarrassing her. And to me, she would have been no less desirable if she'd been eighteen years older than I, instead of eight.

To further develop Ethel's reason for worry about her age, a few lines later she tells Bill she is pregnant:

I almost dropped my cup in my eagerness to reach her. "Honey! That's great!" I gathered her in my arms, suddenly too choked to say anything more. For the first time, she didn't return my embrace, but drew away from me.

"Is it?" she asked, and I realized then the seriousness in her face was actually fear. "Remember, Bill, I'm not eighteen."

I knew it was no picnic to have a baby at any age, and to have a first one at thirty-five could be downright dangerous. I tried to kiss away her fears and insisted she would have the best doctor, the best care money could buy.

"That's not what I'm thinking about," she said quietly, running her fingers through my hair. "In a couple of months, you'll be ashamed of me. I'll be so ugly in those awful dresses and flat shoes, and maybe—maybe I'll stay fat and out of shape . . . ."

"Not you, honey!" I laughed, hoping to change her mood. "That's for gals who haven't any pride and didn't have a good figure to begin with!"

"My mother was thirty-eight when I was born. It made her look forty-eight," Ethel said in a strangely tense, quiet voice.

I spent the next two TV programs convincing her nothing could change my love—not if she looked one hundred and eight.

Please note that I did not have little Karen get run over, or come down with a fatal illness during one of her mother's drinking orgies, to make Ethel "come to realize" she needed professional help. I had the child so worried and concerned about her mother's headaches and frequent days of not feeling well that she played poorly at a piano recital. She embarrassed herself, her teacher—and her mother. It was seeing and feeling the agony the child experienced on the stage during the recital that made Ethel come to realize she was ruining all their lives, and aware that she must do something about it.

To prepare the reader for the recital, I used the following narrative:

All parents brag about their youngster's talents, but it was Karen's piano teacher who bragged the most.

When Karen was eight, Miss Allison said our daughter had unusual possibilities as a pianist. She spent all of her spare time practicing her piano lessons, until she began to worry about her mother's headaches.

Remember, the reader must always feel sympathetic toward the "sinner." To let the reader better understand Ethel and to like her, I used the following narrative:

As Karen grew older, so did Ethel, so did I. One thing I especially admired about my wife was the fact that she didn't act kittenish around younger people or try to hide the little lines around her eyes with a lot of messy makeup.

All bedroom scenes, or "sex scenes" must have a definite purpose in the story. In the following, I let the reader know what was going on in Ethel's mind—her worry about the difference in her age and her husband's.

One night, after giving herself to me with the same complete abandon that hadn't lessened in the years of our marriage, she lay quietly in my arms. I thought she was asleep until she spoke from the dark. "Bill, when you make love to me, do you ever wish I were—younger?"

"Of course not!" I answered quickly. "When we're both as old as Methuselah, I'll still enjoy holding you in my arms."

And that's all we said. But many nights I felt as if Ethel were trying to prove something. About the same time, I noticed she was drinking too much at parties.

Referring back to the notes on some of the necessary ingredients for a love story, a personal problem or confession magazine story, you will find the "theme vehicle" listed. I gave the Kent's a housekeeper, Mrs. Brandon, who, as the "theme vehicle" does not fight with, control, or dominate any of the main characters. The purpose of the "theme vehicle" is to give more depth to the *theme*, to strengthen the point the author wants to prove in the story. In other words, the "theme vehicle" acts as the author's mouthpiece. Since the point to be proved in this story is that love, patience and understanding win out, I have Mrs. Brandon challenge these attributes of the husband. Farther along in the story is the following scene:

> Mrs. Brandon always held the door open, turned down the bed covers, the nights I carried Ethel in, not saying a word, but bristling with disapproval. I thought her disapproval was directed at my wife, until one night she surprised me by saying, "The missus can't take liquor, so why do you make her go out and drink so much?"
>
> "Make her!" I exploded. "She's not exactly a child, you know. I don't tell her what to do!"
>
> "'Course, I got no business being concerned if you ain't," she went on, "but Mrs. Kent will be sick if she keeps this up. She don't eat nothing all day because of her diet, and just living on liquor ain't healthy for a woman her age."

After several occasions when Karen comes home from school to find her mother out cold, drunk, there are a couple of short scenes in which Bill tries to get Ethel to say why she drinks so much. Each time Ethel promises to stop. Bill is finally forced to recognize the seriousness of the problem.

My patience endured until the evening I came home and Karen greeted me at the door with her finger to her lips. "Shh," she said, "mother's asleep. I guess she had one of those headaches again. She had to take a sleeping pill. She left me a note."

I hurried into the bedroom, knowing what I would find. It was then, while I stood there looking down at her, so pale and beautiful in her deathlike stupor, that despair and panic gripped me. When would this stop? Why had it started? I had to know what I was fighting in order to continue the battle, and I needed help.

I called Dr. Phillips, our family physician and the only person I felt I could ask for advice. Then, in order to get Karen out of the house, I grabbed some shirts from a drawer and told her that Mrs. Brandon was expecting them for mending. When she turned her pale, anxious little face up to me she said, "Are you sure she's okay, Daddy?" I held her close to me for a moment, too choked up to say anything. Oh, Ethel, I thought, if you could see the look on your child's face this minute, or know the adult burden of worry and fear you're forcing her to bear, you'd never touch another drop!

I had just finished telling Mrs. Brandon on the telephone to keep Karen there awhile when the doctor arrived. Without a word between us, I took him up to Ethel. He walked over to the bed and pulled her eyelids back, then held his stethoscope to her chest, and next, he counted her pulse. "Well?" I blurted impatiently.

"Well what, Mr. Kent?" he asked quietly. "Your wife's an alcoholic. She'll be all right when she sleeps it off."

An alcoholic! That's what I had expected him to say. I dropped into a chair beside the bed. An alcoholic! But why? Why? I must have said it out loud because the doctor shrugged and said, "The menopause affects all women differently. Some become temporarily unbalanced; others run away from those they love and try to lose their identity in the world; a lot of well-adjusted women simply become nervous and irritable for a time, then some try to lose themselves in alcohol. It depends on the person's state of mind."

The menopause? But that was impossible! "But Ethel—she's so . . . so . . . ."

He interrupted me. "So young?" He followed my glance to Ethel's softly curved body outlined beneath the silk spread before he added, "Sometimes it comes as early as forty or as late as fifty. Mrs. Kent, as you know, is forty-four."

I felt strangely freed of a vast burden. "Well, if that's all, then let's get on the ball!" I cried enthusiastically. "Let's give her some shots or whatever you give women at such times!"

"I have been giving Mrs. Kent shots," Dr. Phillips said patiently, closing his little black bag.

"You have?" I asked, knowing it sounded stupid. "Why wasn't I told about them?"

"It isn't unusual for a woman not to want to discuss this working of nature with her husband," he said. "It does something to their vanity, discovering they are no longer fertile. They see themselves as suddenly no longer desirable as a woman." His eyes swept over my six foot frame and settled on my face. "In Mrs. Kent's case," he added, "I imagine it was doubly difficult."

I felt the flush creep into my cheeks. I was about to declare I had never given her any reason to be concerned with the difference in our ages, but he didn't give me a chance. "I know what you're going to say, Bill, but the female mind is complex and hard to understand."

"But look, doc," I began, feeling desperate again, "whatever the reason, can't we do something? There's medicine, cures—I've read about them!"

"How long do you think a compulsory cure lasts, Bill?" Then, without waiting for me to answer, he went on. "Just as long as it takes to go from the hospital to the liquor store on the way home!" At the door he offered his hand. "Don't think I'm being unsympathetic, Bill," he said, "but there's nothing to be done unless you can convince Mrs. Kent to help herself."

After more promises by Ethel not to drink—a week of sobriety in which she sews a dress for Karen's recital—the big night arrives. Bill finds the girl sitting alone and worried in a corner of the recital hall because her mother has not arrived. He rushes home and gets Ethel out of bed and puts her under the cold shower until she sobers up, then he makes her get dressed and takes her to the auditorium. But too late for Karen to know they are there, watching and listening. Which brings us to the scene:

I don't believe I ever had such a sinking feeling as at that moment. "Poor little kid," I said aloud.

I felt Ethel's cold fingers clutch my hand. "Oh, Bill—she's doing terrible!"

"That's putting it mildly," I said. "She doesn't even know she's up there. Mentally she's home, trying to awaken her mother to get dressed for the biggest occasion of her eight years." At home, when Karen played the entire room vibrated with the thunderous chords; she had such unusually strong hands. But now, her playing sounded like a bunch of nothing, just memorized notes. She looked so small, so forlorn at the huge piano. She kept her head down, as if studying each key before she struck it.

"She knows it perfectly. Why is she playing so poorly?" Ethel whispered, and I realized she hadn't heard me. My heart ached for Karen, for what she was feeling. I had to swallow the thickness in my throat before I could speak.

"I promised her we would stand in the wings, so she could see you and know you were okay. She was worried . . . ."

When Ethel didn't say anything, I looked around. She was huddled against the door frame. It was dark, but I knew she was crying.

Then follows the scene in which the three of them start home, with the mother trying to comfort the child. Next is a scene in the parents' bedroom. Ethel pleads with Bill to give her another chance. She tries to convince Bill she does love her daughter, and him. He is not convinced. She has broken too many promises to him. She finally tells him her mother had not died a natural death, but had taken her own life because her young and handsome husband had left her for a younger woman, She takes a snapshot from a drawer and hands it to Bill:

> "There!" she said, and thrust the picture out to me. "This is the reason I started drinking! That's my mother when I was five years old. I drank whiskey to forget—to forget that some day I would look like that, too."

During the rest of this scene, Ethel goes into detail about her parents. She reveals now why she was worried Bill would desert her. Here, in detail, the problem is brought into focus; the problem that developed in a woman's mind when she married a man younger than herself. After Ethel has opened her heart and soul to her husband, the story moves on toward the conclusion. This major scene is the "obligatory scene," in which the main character, the one who has done wrong in the story, vindicates himself (or herself)—in this case, Ethel. This scene is also used to reveal the author's philosophy concerning the theme, or the story's main problem, whether it be one of premarital sex, dope addiction, conniving for success on a job—or, as in this case, a philosophy concerning a man's love for a woman despite her age.

The "obligatory scene" continues:

> I was so filled with relief that I pulled her into my arms. "Oh, my poor darling, why should I resent the work of nature? Every woman born goes through the same thing you are undergoing. And what happened between your parents happens every day somewhere in the world. Age isn't the reason. It's the person. Your

father would have done the same thing if he had been ten years older than your mother!"

"I imagine that's what her friends tried to tell her, but she didn't believe it."

"She didn't believe it because she didn't want to admit she chose the wrong partner. But we didn't make her mistake, Ethel," I said. "I love you very, very much. I couldn't imagine my life with anyone but you. That's why I couldn't bear seeing you ruin your health."

"I know that now, Bill, but I never felt absolutely sure of it. I wouldn't let myself be sure of it or believe your love for me and your child was strong enough to stay with us forever, until tonight in the auditorium when I saw you suffer for poor little Karen. I realized then you could only be so terribly hurt because you loved us both so very much."

She stopped and stared long and hard at the picture she took from me, as if seeing it for the first time. "It's a pity she didn't see him as he really was. She had no reason to die," she said thoughtfully. "Neither did I have any reason to drink. Now it's too late . . . ."

All the things I had said to her since taking the corsage to Karen raced through my mind, and I was ashamed. It was a relief to know why she drank, but knowing wouldn't stop it. It had gone too far for that.

"It's never too late for anything, Ethel," I said, believing the words. "When two people love each other as much as we do, things are bound to work out all right!"

"I could go to Miami Hospital in Springfield for a cure," Ethel suggested.

"They say it's hell, Ethel, pure unadulterated hell," I warned.

"I know," she said resignedly. "But there was something else I discovered tonight in the auditorium. I had to prove to you and Karen that I loved you both and that I was worth another chance. Please, take me, Bill, now! It's only thirty miles."

I pressed my lips to hers. I tried to say with my kiss all the things I couldn't put into words. Then I went to the phone and called Mrs. Brandon to come to stay with Karen.

It was four-thirty in the afternoon when I signed the papers admitting my wife to Miami, exactly one year ago. It was one long, horrible, gut-twisting nightmare of agony for Ethel. But now it is all over.

The problem has been solved, the story basically ended, but following the above there was approximately 350 words of "summation." It added nothing new to the philosophy or to the theme. The point already had been proven; that love, patience and understanding can correct most marriage problems. But this final paragraph served to relax the reader who, hopefully, had lived the story with the characters.

My story "Abortion In The Back Seat," published in *Thrilling Confessions*, is told from the male viewpoint. It also originated from an overheard comment. A high school boy who sat across the aisle from me on a bus remarked to his friend that he was "scared to death of his girlfriend's father; that he would never give them permission to marry after graduation because he said they were too young for marriage."

I thought about those two young people, in love but unable to marry. Suppose with today's permissiveness they decided not to wait for marriage? What would the young man do if he learned their lovemaking had left the girl pregnant? The reader of my story wanted to know the answers to these questions, and the solutions to the situation which was ultimately reached.

Here is how I handled it:

I motivated the main story by use of flashback to tell the reader the events that had led to the creation of the problem, and defined the problem.

The next Saturday night when I knew Wendy was going to baby sit at the same place, I asked her if it was all right if I could come over and watch TV with her. After that I went every Saturday night. The Evanses belonged to a bowling team. I asked Wendy in the beginning if she'd gotten permission from Mrs. Evans to have somebody in the house with her, [this is to show Gary was a pretty nice kid] and she said Mrs. Evans said it'd be okay with her if Wendy's folks said so. But Wendy knew they'd never allow it, so she didn't tell them. I know it was wrong, but I'd go there after the little boy was asleep, and I always left an hour before the Evanses were due back home.

I wanted to be with Wendy all the time. Like I said, she was my girl and those Saturday nights together were our dates. We'd watch TV nights she didn't have homework to catch up on. We'd hug and kiss, and I'd sweet talk her, but that's all I ever did. I was old enough to know that if I wasn't careful, necking could get out of hand. I'd heard talk from a couple of the boys at school who went all the way with their girls.

Wendy and I had sort of a silent agreement that we'd wait until we got married to do anything. Maybe it was just that we were so scared of her old man, I don't know. Anyway, I never thought about anything but necking with her in the Evans house.

Besides, I was on pins and needles most of the time. I always felt uneasy, and every time I'd hear a car stop or voices out front, I'd jump up and want to run, afraid they'd get sore if they found me there. Once little Tommy woke up, and I had to hide in the kitchen closet until she got him back to sleep, and I thought I'd smother to death.

Then the Saturday night of Halloween week, when I got to the house, Wendy said, "Well, this is one night you won't have to run, sweetie. We can watch the late show if you want." She told me there was a big party going on for the bowling team and the Evanses said they probably wouldn't get home until one o'clock and she could sleep on the divan if she wanted to. to.

We watched TV for a while. Then Wendy suggested we go out in the kitchen and have a snack. Because they were going to be so late, they'd left food for her to make sandwiches.

"This is fun," she said, putting the plates on the table, "just like it was our house and we were married and had to be quiet so we didn't wake the baby."

I thought it was really nice. I pretended right along with her. I kept calling her Mrs. Elliot and she'd call me Mr. Elliot. Every time she passed me something, I'd reach over and kiss her. When we got done in the kitchen, she suggested we go play some records for a while, until the late show came on.

I never was much of a dancer, and Wendy said this was a good time for me to learn. So we danced. And all of a sudden, holding her in my arms like that, she was so little and so warm and cuddly I hugged her real tight and kissed her.

We'd kissed lots and lots of times, but this was different. I felt so grown up toward her. Maybe it was all the playing house bit. I told her how much I loved her, that she was the only girl in the world I ever wanted. The music was so soft, and we only had the one small lamp on. Then the record ended, and I don't know how, but there we were, on the couch, still in each other's arms.

She sort of whispered against my face, "I love you so much, Gary. I wish we were married now."

And I don't know but before I realized what I was doing, I had eased her down on the cushions and was making love to her. When it was over, I was trembling, and I was scared, and I felt ashamed because I hadn't controlled myself like I always said I could.

Wendy started to cry. "We were going to wait until we got married," she said. "Now you won't think I'm a nice girl."

I hugged her tight to stop the shaking in my body, and I told her I'd always think she was a nice girl, that she was a wonderful girl, my little sweetheart.

"We won't do this any more until we're married, okay Gary?" she said, and I agreed with her. I said we would forget tonight, pretend it never happened.

This rather mild "sex scene" is used as background for the story; to prepare the reader for the *result* of that encounter which becomes the actual problem of the story: Wendy's ultimate pregnancy, and Gary's decision to perform an abortion in the back seat of his car, which is made logical or believable to the reader by indicating Gary's intensive study of medical books on the female anatomy. Then the story continues:

"Don't worry, honey, everything's going to be okay," I said, and told her what I was going to do. She just sat there, looking at me. She didn't say anything. "You're not afraid to let me, are you, Wendy?" I finally asked her.

"I guess not," she said so soft I could hardly hear her. "But won't it hurt? Alma said the man would put me to sleep so I don't feel anything. You think it'll hurt, Gary?" she asked me again.

I didn't know if it would hurt or not, but I told her the reason he'd put her to sleep first was like in the movies, so she couldn't tell on him later. Then I remembered Mom's sleeping pills.

"They're safe, Wendy," I explained. "They're the kind you can buy in the drug store without a prescription. You'll just go to sleep, and I'll do it while you're asleep. Then you won't feel anything."

We made arrangements for her to slip out of her house after her folks were asleep. I was going to do the same, and I'd pick her up at the corner by the library. She had a key to her kitchen door and would get back in without them knowing it.

I don't know how I got through that day. Friday nights Mom set up the ironing board in the living room and ironed while she and Aunt Effy watched TV—and tonight it seemed like she was ironing a ton of stuff. I thought she'd never get through and Aunt Effy go home, so Mom would go up to bed. Every time I checked Harry's door, his light was on until almost midnight. When the house was finally dark, I still had to wait a while to make sure they were both asleep.

I rolled my car down the driveway to the street, so I wouldn't have to start it near the house. I had Harry's bag in the trunk. I even had a pop bottle of water for Wendy to take the sleeping pills with.

She ran out from the shadows of the library when I got to the curb. It was cold and she was shivering. Neither one of us said anything, and I headed out to Balboa Park. Then I gave her the bottle of pills and the water. I turned on the dash light and told her to read what it said to take.

"It says take two, but I might wake up while you're doing it, maybe you'll hurt me," Wendy said, and I told her to go ahead and take three; it couldn't be dangerous because anybody could buy them at the drugstore. If they were dangerous they wouldn't be allowed to sell them.

While I drove along I went over everything in my mind that I was going to do. Wendy just sat there, looking out the window. It took about twenty minutes to get to the picnic grounds. I yawned a couple of times. I hadn't had much sleep the past two days. I held tight to the wheel because my hands kept wanting to shake.

We'd just reached the row of pine trees when I felt her slump over against my shoulder. And suddenly, I felt alone. I felt like I was out there all by myself, because I called her name and she didn't answer me. She was asleep already. I pulled up to a spot off the road and shut off the motor. When I got out of the car I eased Wendy's head down on the seat and straightened her out. Then I hurried around back to get the things from the trunk. I had my big camping flashlight I intended to rig up on the car door.

I stood at the open car door and unzipped the bag. With the flashlight in one hand, I took out the things I needed. Somehow, the light hit the metal of that instrument in a wierd way. My stomach went up in knots. I threw the thing back in the bag. I turned the flashlight on Wendy's face. She looked like a little kid, sleeping like that, with her long hair all mussed up on her shoulders . . . .

[Here starts the "obligatory" scene, when Gary begins to *vindicate* himself.]

How awful. Oh my God, Wendy, how awful, was all I could think. All of a sudden I seemed to come to, to snap out of a fog I'd been in. I kept turning the flashlight first on her, then on that black bag, trying to figure it all out. "Oh, Wendy, Wendy, what was I going to do? How could I be so crazy? How could I be so nutty . . . .?" I kept talking to hear the sound of my voice. It was so black outside. So awfully quiet.

How crazy—how crazy can a guy get? I might have

killed Wendy, poking that thing up in her—and if she had a little baby started, *I wasn't God*—I couldn't say it should die, *just because I was afraid of her old man!*

I ran around and threw the bag in the trunk, then I got in the front seat. I shook Wendy, hard. "Don't you worry, honey; don't you worry a bit—everything's going to be okay!" I told her, but she didn't wake up. I backed that car out onto the road, and I really burned rubber getting out of there.

Because in that split second I knew what I was going to do—and nobody was going to stop me! And I couldn't understand now why I hadn't decided to do it in the first place. I was going to drive over to Greene County and park in front of the Justice of the Peace office until it opened at eight o'clock in Greenfield. I would lie about my age. In Greene County you didn't have to get a marriage license first—the JP took care of everything.

It was almost 80 miles to Greenfield. My car was old and I couldn't go very fast. I didn't want to drive fast in case a cop was out on the road. I didn't want anybody or anything to stop me until I was married to Wendy. Her old man could do what he wanted to. Now, while I rode along in the dark, I thought what a stupid ass I'd been, to be afraid of her father. What could he do but beat me up. He wouldn't kill me; or would he? Anyway, he wouldn't do anything until I married Wendy. It'd work out, somehow.

I reached over and pulled her coat up closer to her neck. It was cold and I didn't have a heater. I thought, how could a girl love a guy who was scared of her old man. Maybe she didn't really love me—maybe she thought I was a coward; she didn't love me at all and that was why she was willing for me to do that awful thing to her.

That was the longest 80 miles I ever drove in my life, and it didn't help any to have the kind of thoughts I had. If Mom looked in my room and saw I wasn't there, she'd call the police.

Finally I was on Main Street in Greenfield. I knew about where the JP's office was, near the court house. I'd come over here with Harry to get the papers for my car.

Nothing ever looked so good to me as that sign: *Fred Beehman, Justice of the Peace.* I took one great big sigh of relief, then I shut off the motor and settled down to wait.

I fell asleep, because I woke up, shaking from the cold. My feet felt frozen; they were stiff. It was daylight. Outside, the air was that funny grey before the sun comes up. I stretched out my arms—they were so cold and sore and stiff. When I moved, Wendy toppled over, against the car door. She looked so funny I called her name. She didn't answer me and I thought, of course, she would still be asleep; it hadn't been eight hours since she took the sleeping pills.

I pulled her back against me and she felt so funny, so limp, so lifeless. I turned up her face and lifted her eyelids to wake her up. I kept patting her cheek. But she didn't move or anything. She acted like she was dead.

I panicked. I thought, oh, my God, she's dead. It was then I saw the bottle of sleeping pills on the floor. I picked it up. It was empty, and it had been half full when I gave it to her. She'd been so scared I was going to hurt her she'd taken them all. I felt her pulse and I kept begging over and over, please, please, don't be dead; please wake up; *please wake up!*

I finally imagined I felt a bit of pulse. I looked up and down the street to see if there was any building that looked like a hospital. I turned the key but the motor wouldn't start because it was cold, and I was shaking so bad. I was scared and kept flooding the engine. The street was empty so I couldn't flag anybody down. Then finally I got the car going. I drove on down Main Street, looking for an open filling station so I could find out where a hospital was, but nothing was open.

I kept driving and, on impulse, I laid on the horn. I took a right turn on Walker Street, driving slow, my hand still on the horn. And it worked. I heard a siren and I saw the red light in my rear view mirror. I pulled to the curb and stopped. I didn't wait for the cop to come to me. I got out of that car and ran to him and told him I had to get to a hospital quick. My girl was sick, maybe she was dead, but please to help me.

"Okay buddy, get going—I'll lead," he said, without any questions. Before I was back in my seat, he was up in front of me, his siren going again. And that was the most wonderful sound in the world.

Those first minutes in the Emergency Ward were terrible. But that cop was a great guy. When I couldn't get words out he filled in, and they got working on Wendy immediately. It was too late to pump her stomach; it'd been too long ago she took the pills, but they gave her some shots and they walked her and I don't know what all they did while I sat in the lobby sweating it out. And the policeman was there, too. At this point, I guess, he wanted to see I didn't run out.

He knew who I was from my driver's license. I'd told him we were going to get married; we were trying to sleep in front of the JP's to wait for morning. He was the one who told the Emergency doctor he guessed Wendy had taken the sleeping pills so she could sleep in the cold, sitting up. Or maybe this is what I told him while we were getting Wendy out of the car; I don't remember.

Well, by noon her folks were there. They thought we'd had a car accident and that was the reason Wendy was in the hospital. Mr. Doliver looked about, ready to explode when he came stomping down that hospital corridor and saw me. "You little bum, I'm going to kill you for this!" he said before he even got close to me. Mrs. Doliver looked sick and worried, but she kept trying to quiet him. But nothing would stop him. "I'm going to break every bone in your body!" he roared at me, and he had my sweater pulled up tight at my throat and I could hardly breathe. *"But first you're going to marry that girl*—soon as she's able," he said. Then, while he raved on, it dawned on me he was *insisting* I had to marry Wendy because I had ruined her reputation by keeping her out all night!

I tried to talk to him, but he wouldn't give me a chance. Finally I yanked away and yelled, *"Shut up and listen to me!"* Then I told him that was what I intended to do—that was why we were in Greenfield, to get married.

Once the words started, I couldn't stop them. I

ignored the nurse when she came up and motioned to be quiet. Mr. Doliver just stood there, looking at me. I told him I didn't care what he did to me. I loved Wendy. We wanted to get married. *We had to get married.* But we'd been afraid of him. Wendy was scared to death of him, but *I* wasn't any more!

"You hear me? *I'm not afraid of you anymore!* We'll get along," I said. Mrs. Doliver came over and put her arm around me and she motioned to Wendy's father to sit down on the bench.

"Let's act like civilized people," she said. Just then the doctor came out in the hall. Wendy's folks jumped up and the doctor motioned for them to sit back down. "No, not right now. She just wants Gary. Let him go in alone," he said, and I did.

Now we have arrived at what is termed the "thematic conclusion." Here the main point of the story is proved and the reason or purpose for the story being written is made clear to the reader.

Well, I could go on all about what everybody did and said, but it all boils down to one thing. Wendy and I got married that next Saturday, at the Minister's house, with her folks' signed consent on the license. They got her a pretty new outfit, and Harry got Mom a new dress too.

Mr. Mason, the Principal, made a special request to the school board for me to finish and graduate. Of course, Wendy had to quit. The Dolivers talked it over with Mom and Harry and between them they decided it'd be best for us to live at my house. Wendy could help Mom a lot and soon Harry would be leaving to go back to school, and we could use his room for a nursery.

Wendy and I just let them plan it all the way they wanted it, because we knew we'd better quit while we were ahead. At least we were smart enough to realize we couldn't make it on our own. We did need help, lots of it for a long time, and we were lucky our two families were offering it to us, so we had to take it the way they dished it out.

The hardest thing for me was going back to school Monday, because the newspapers really played it up big, and sort of ugly. One paper even said it was a suicide pact, but I chickened out, then got scared and tried to save Wendy. They said I should be in jail.

Well, about one thing they were right. I did "chicken out," but to keep from taking another life, not my own.

The messages for the readers (or morals) are now obvious: Baby sitters should not entertain boyfriends while on duty, but if they do they should be aware of the consequences of "playing house" realistically. Even normally well-behaved teenagers are rarely emotionally mature enough to cope with the possible developments from premarital sex.

6

DRAMA IN EVERYDAY LIFE

Perhaps, having read the preceding chapters, you are thinking nothing *that* dramatic ever happens to you.

"I've lived such a commonplace, routine kind of life it wouldn't make an interesting story . . . ," you tell yourself, forgetting that it is how one deals with life, whether commonplace or dramatic, that is the foundation of all stories, fact or fiction.

Let's take an example: You are a young man in his early twenties. Your name is Joe Fairland. You graduated from high school somewhat to the surprise of your parents, and took a job with a trucking company. In time you met *the* girl. Her name was Lillie. You went to parties together and you took her on picnics, with some pretty heavy necking sessions when you were alone. You wanted to "go all the way," declaring over and over that you loved her and "having each other now" wouldn't make any difference.

But Lillie was devout about sex. She wanted to be a virgin when she married, and wear the traditional white wedding gown. If you hadn't known you were in love with Lillie before, you knew it now. She was everything you wanted in a wife, beautiful, eager, *and virtuous*. And so you were married. Then came the awakening. You couldn't talk to friends and neighbors about your problem so you wrote about it to a magazine editor.

All the time I was going with Lillie she was a doll. She smelled good and looked pretty. When we went to parties with our friends she always did her hair in a cute way. Her legs were exciting, especially in nylons and high-heel slippers, and her dresses fit nice and showed she was built the way a woman should be. After we got married I discovered she liked to sleep "in the raw," and that really got me going. Sex with Lillie was *something*! We used to go to a motel on Saturday nights a couple of times a month to keep things as exciting as our honeymoon. She'd meet me at the end of my Cleveland to Columbus run, and we'd make it like a real "hot" date all weekend. I even changed my truck runs so I wouldn't ever be away from her overnight, or at least not more than one night if I had to take on another driver's run.

Things went on like that for about three months. Then Lillie starts letting herself get frumpy. She'd smear her face at night with greasy creams and do her hair up in those damn plastic curlers. When I asked her "how come," she said she had to look good because she had a job now. I blew up at that piece of news. I didn't want my wife working; there wasn't any need for her to work. I earned enough to take good care of us.

"But I get lonely, bored, hanging around the house all day," she insisted.

I could see how that could be true. Lillie was too pretty to want to spend her days waiting for me to come home from my run just to have dinner ready.

"All right, honey. Maybe for a while . . . ." I said, but I had a plan.

We had talked about wanting children, and how many. Now was a good time to start makin' that dream come true. Pretty soon Lillie was so pregnant she couldn't wear her pretty clothes to work and was satisfied to stay home. And that led to our biggest problem.

When she got bored she ate. Everything in sight. The doctor gave her a special diet which she'd follow carefully, then cram herself between meals. She got as big as the truck I was drivin', and lazy. She didn't bother puttin' on lipstick or doing her hair up pretty. She didn't even use the curlers any more, which was a blessing in one way but it didn't do anything for her looks at the supper table—or the breakfast table. I tried to be helpful and understanding. Having to go through all she was to have my baby, the least I could do was not make a big thing of the way she looked. Everything would be back to the way it was that first month as soon as our little Joey was born. Except that Lillie wouldn't have time then to be bored or lonely while I was working.

But things didn't get better. They got worse. A lot worse.

Lillie went back to the curlers but now she wore 'em day *and* night. While she was pregnant she said she was "eating for two" when I mentioned that she wasn't sticking to the doctor's diet. Now she still ate for two, both of 'em herself. She didn't even nurse Joey; said her milk lacked something or other. The house was never neat anymore the way she kept it that first month or two, and she wouldn't do the grocery shopping without I went along and carried the baby. Joey cried if someone didn't carry him.

The first time she pulled this on me she looked like something made up to scare kids. Her hair was in big roller-curlers, no makeup, either. She was so fat now she had to wear "mother-hubbards," them tent-like things my grandmother used to wear because she couldn't get into anything else. I blew up again, something I didn't do very often.

"Oh, no you don't! You won't get me on the street with you lookin' the way you do."

She started yellin' at me, sayin' things like it was all my fault—the baby, how fat she was, and the way her feet hurt so she had to wear carpetslippers instead of shoes. And then she waddled over to the dresser and got a scarf and tied it around her head, which only made her look worse. I knew if I didn't go with her to buy the groceries I'd probably have to eat supper at the hamburger stand down the street. I went along with her.

That's my beef, Madame Editor. Can't you publish some stories about guys like us? I loved Lillie when we was married. I still do in a way. I never cheat on her or make passes at cute chicks like the other drivers do when we stop for coffee on the drive. But I can't go on like this much longer. Them cute waitresses are lookin' more desirable every day!

Maybe you could start a crusade or something to tell wives they ought to keep lookin' nice *after* marriage, too, because that's even more important than *before* marriage. A man don't expect his wife to go on bein' a glamour girl all the time when she's got kids to take care of. But it sure would be nice if she'd put on a decent dress and take them darned curlers outa her hair before he comes home to supper.

Joe's story, as I'm sure you've discovered by this time, is the basis for several stories in this category because it is also the "beef" of hundreds, even thousands of husbands; and in reverse, that of many wives with husbands who hate to shave, get haircuts, or dress up for a neighbor's party. Joe's problem is also the *reason* behind the unfaithfulness of some husbands, or wives, which may lead to complications far beyond those Joe experienced, even murder.

The point emphasized here is that once you know the "rules" of the writing game and the basic facts about construction, motivation, purpose, theme, etc., you can make a story from even the simplest or seemingly uneventful life.

Consider a few possibilities for Joe's story. Suppose the wife turned all her love to her child and began to hate her husband, or at least to ignore him most of the time. Sexual relations were strained, then vanished altogether. Joe began playing around, Lillie, in revenge, said "what was sauce for the goose, the gander could enjoy too," and began having afternoon affairs with anyone conveniently at hand—salesmen, deliverymen, and the like—and discovered that some men like their women with a lot of meat on their bones. What would this do to the child? The variations are endless once you know how to put a story together.

Joe took the easy way to try to solve his problem—asking an editor to do it for him. Don't make that mistake. Editors buy stories; they don't publish them simply because a reader offers one free. Write your story and submit it to a confession magazine editor. If you follow the rules set forth in this book, the chances are you'll hear from the editor. And if it is an interesting story which appeals to a wide reader audience but still needs improvement, often the editor will suggest changes needed and will reconsider your story when you have improved it.

Obviously Joe's story as presented here is not complete. What he did about his problem or how he solved it still must be determined. You might use his experience (which may also be similar to your own) as an "exercise in writing." See how many ways you could logically and convincingly conclude Joe's story (or your own) and solve the problem.

You may find that the problem in this story can be told more effectively from the woman's viewpoint. If so, you must get into Lillie's heart and mind, know what made her change as she did. You must suffer with her when she begins to realize her husband is growing cold toward her, coming home late, avoiding parties which he used to enjoy, is not wanting to "show her off" to his friends any more. Now he never compliments her about anything, but is always making admiring remarks about so-and-so's wife or girlfriend. When Lillie can stand it no longer, she confronts her husband, accuses him of infidelity. There is a stormy scene. She tells him their marriage is finished, she's leaving him!

Here you have the basic elements of the story: Lillie has "sinned" by letting herself become a slob; she has suffered in believing Joe no longer loves her and is unfaithful; now she must repent and *vindicate* herself.

Lillie decides to take the baby and go to her mother. She intends to get a job, be self-supporting again. Her mother will take care of the baby, but Lillie can't expect her to feed and clothe them too. The first "slap in the face" Lillie encounters is when she opens the closet door to pack her clothes. Here are all the pretty dresses, slacks, blouses, and high-heeled shoes which she wore while working in an office and dating Joe. The mirror on the closet door shows her what she looks like now. But Lillie is not yet ready to "repent." She crams a few things into a suitcase, packs some of the baby's clothes, and leaves for her mother's house.

The mother now becomes the *theme vehicle.*

Her mother is surprised to see her and obviously shocked by her appearance, but she doesn't comment on this now. But Lillie is aware of how nice her mother looks. Neatly dressed, with a fresh hairdo, her mother looks younger by twenty years than she does! She shrugs this off by telling her mother she knows she looks "a fright" but . . . and blames Joe for the way she looks. Now, she says, she'll have time to look after herself once in a while—get her hair done, some new clothes and shoes, and have spending money of her own.

The mother makes no reply at this point, but after a day or two she talks frankly to her daughter; tells her that if she had done all those things months ago—hairdos, nice clothes, etc.—she wouldn't be running away from her husband or thinking he was unfaithful, and if he was, whose fault was that?

At first Lillie is resentful of criticism she knows is just. Her mother reasons with her, makes her see that the more unhappy one is with herself the more likely she is to overeat in compensation; which leads to overweight and a whole bagful of other problems. She shows Lillie a picture of herself three years ago. "You looked like that then, you can look that way again if you are willing to work for what you want—your figure, your home and husband and child."

Lillie now sincerely repents. She asks her mother to call Joe and tell him they are going to take a little trip together, and will be back in a week or so. And not to mind Lillie's temper; she needs a little time to come to her senses. Lillie uses that time to start making herself over, back to what she was when Joe married her; maybe not as cute, but definitely a woman who cares about herself, her husband and child.

There are, of course, variations of the conclusion, and it must not be as simple as it sounds here. Lillie must get a few more rebuffs—maybe see her husband out with another girl and think getting him back is hopeless—before the tide of their affairs begins to turn. Then let something unexpected happen, maybe some simple little event which would not have been significant under other circumstances, to make both realize that they still love each other; that she needed only to show that love by keeping herself loveable.

Often what seems a trivial problem can cause more serious problems by allowing it to grow out of all proportions. Many marriages have been destroyed by something as trivial at the outset as Lillie's carelessness over her appearance.

Your own personal problem need not come from the same reason Joe's did; or Lillie's. But it can be a small thing, nothing world-shaking at the outset. A money problem; a new job with a troublesome boss; an interfering "well-meaning" friend; a possessive mother (or father) or a busybody mother-in-law or father-in-law. Always strive for some original treatment of your story, but don't overdo that, as we have warned earlier in this book. For instance, the mother-in-law interference is slightly overworked in stories. Let it be someone else who interferes; or perhaps do a switch to a mother-in-law who *doesn't* interfere enough.

Suppose you are a husband who has to help with the housework because your wife is always tired, or not feeling well. You talk to your neighbor about the situation while he's mowing his lawn.

"I don't know what's got into Carrie lately. Here I am on my only day off and I've got to hang up the damn wash," you complain. You think your wife is turning into a lazy slob, but you don't say that to Harry. But you do continue to gripe about things. "What in hell these women do all week I don't know. One of these days I'm going to put my foot down. Carrie's gettin' broad as a truck . . . . "

Harry nods and says, yeah, he's noticed.

You are not the only husband who resents having to do house work on your day off and thinks it is about time to "do something about it." What to do is the problem.

You can help yourself, and other husbands in the same fix, by writing your problem into a story for a confession magazine. However, don't make it one long gripe. To get readers' sympathy, you must sound like an average home loving husband. Through your story you must advise and guide, help other husbands to find their own answers to similar problems. No two problems are exactly alike. What you did about your problem might not be possible for someone else in just the same way, but your solution may provide the direction and stamina he needed.

An important point to remember in writing for today's readers is that it is not merely *what* your characters do in a story, but *why* they do it. Psychiatrists are not as concerned with the fact that teenage John is on heroin as in finding out why he turned to drugs. When a doctor treats a young girl or boy for overindulgence in sex he wants to know first why overindulgence is necessary. When a man commits himself to a hospital for treatment for alcoholism it is very important that the doctor first find out what started him drinking to excess.

Let's go back to Carrie's story for a moment. You cannot offer a logical solution to the husband's problem unless you know why Carrie has become a slovenly housewife. In this story the husband may find that he has misjudged Carrie's reasons for fatigue and neglecting their home. Now he would want to "make amends," *vindicate* himself. But he wouldn't discover the reason for his wife's "laziness" without some searching, some suspicion that he has misjudged her. He sends her to a doctor for a complete physical and learns that she is really ill. (Do not make this some incurable or rare disease.) And don't over-dramatize. Let the illness be something not uncommon to average people, something that can be cured with proper treatment in a reasonable time, plus *love and patience*. These are important elements in the solution of most problems.

In other words, be a creative writer with balance for the kind of story you are writing. And remember that all love stories do *not* have to have big sex scenes. Emotion, yes, and understanding and patience, which imply a happy sexual relationship.

7

THE SHORT STORY VS THE NOVELETTE

Confession magazines, as you have learned by this time, buy stories which fall into one or the other of two categories in length: the short story or the novelette. Since the pay for such stories is by the word, you probably ask yourself "Why write a short story when I can get more money for a novelette?"

The answer is based on a good deal more than the number of words written.

A short story is less complex in theme and treatment; therefore it requires fewer words to present and make convincing with emotional impact.

A novelette requires more word-length because it is usually two basic stories interwoven. It is also a story with more depth; more need for the author to probe for the causes and effects of actions long endured, or spontaneously taken.

For example, let's go back to a story plot mentioned earlier. A young girl of eighteen has a child out of wedlock. She decides to call herself a widow to avoid the stigma against her child. All goes well at first. She continues to live at her parents' home, starts a new job, and believes she has begun a new life. Then the child's father comes back into her life through a chance encounter.

The first part of the story (novelette) deals with the "cause" events. The second part deals with handling the new and unexpected situation. Of course, the story can take many twists in plot development. These can be emotional or inner adjustments in overcoming the problems which led to the present one; or there may be other complications such as one or the other now being in love with someone else, yet both concerned for their child. Decide what conclusion-theme you want to develop and hold to it. Don't go off on tangents with events you think may improve the story while all they do is clutter it. Discipline is one of the first rules in becoming a successful writer. Plan your story well before you start writing, then stick to the plan. If, when the story is finished, you feel you can substitute a more original event for one you have used, and can do that without disrupting your theme and development, there is no reason why you can't do it. Just keep in mind that a wordy story can also become a "boring" story, regardless of its dramatic plot.

It seems fitting to mention here what we term the "therapy" story. For the most part, these stories are written primarily to "get something off your chest," rather than for money. Many psychiatrists recommend this as a good way to continue treating a mental problem once the patient has brought it under control through professional methods. If resentment against someone or something is "driving you up a wall," spew it all out in words on paper. Get it out of your system! Perhaps you are, unconsciously—like a woman friend of mine who used to write me long letters every week telling me over and over "What bums men are, especially the jerk I married . . . ." Then she would go on about wishing she could find some way to get out of the mess she was in because of that no-good bum . . . and the way he mistreated her (there was always some new insult or cruelty recounted in detail). At first I was sympathetic, then realized that she actually *enjoyed* being a "martyr." If her husband ever tried to leave her she would fight tooth and nail to hold on to him—and to her fancied miseries. I doubt if "therapy writing" could ever solve her problem, but had she been willing to write it honestly, it might have helped others to avoid similar faults.

Another kind of writer who fits into somewhat this same category is the "guilt complex" writer. Such writers have a "deep dark secret" about some "sin" he or she has committed in the past. These writers don't really want to do anything about vindicating themselves, but they want someone to know "what they've been through." So they write their story and send it to an editor. This, in itself, is a kind of confession which eases the individual's guilt at least for a while.

For the writer who wants to write and sell it is perhaps fortunate that most problems people encounter in life are not very different from those his or her neighbors contend with also. Therefore, whatever your problem, it is pretty sure to express much of what someone else is enduring or experiencing and so provides understanding or advice or spiritual uplift for hundreds, even thousands, of other people.

The Ten Commandments give us the *ten basic laws* which may be broken in any story, whether a confession story, a play, a movie, or a novel. Every story written deals with one or more of these *basics*. So you don't need to create some new "sin" for your main character to commit and eventually repent. Use one of the basic sins but *adapt* it to the story you want to write. For instance, a girl can "go wrong" for many reasons and with varied results. A person may break the Commandment "Thou shall have no other gods before Me" in many ways—the worship of money, drinking to excess, dope, women in adultery; all "god" to the indulgent "sinner."

Let's take one final example in more detail: Our character, Hal, is a guilt-complex writer. He cheats on his wife, then tells her about it. Thus he sins and repents, and his conscience is stilled momentarily. But his repentance is not for the sin *committed*, but the fact that he *admitted* it. He titled his story "I Cheated On My Wife":

> I really don't know why I first started stepping out on Mable. Perhaps it was so easy, and she was so trusting and unsuspecting. She loved me and I guess I loved her. We had been married seven years. We had two cute little kids, both boys, Billy—five—and Benny—two.
>
> Mable was still built nice. She was pretty when she fixed up. Sometimes I even think she looked cute in those horrible rollers with that lacy doodad cap over them. I worked four years at Howard's Agency before I was given one afternoon off a week.

The first one I spent at home working in the yard. The next one I asked Mable if she would like to go for a drive somewhere and have a picnic with the kids. She laughed and said, "That's for Sundays, silly, not Wednesdays." So I went down to the YMCA and worked out with a couple of guys.

The third free afternoon I decided to stick around the office and catch up on some correspondence. I told Mable I would stay at work. I was the only one there, so I thought, until little Eadie, the file clerk, came over and asked me if I had change for the cigarette machine.

That's how it started. Just that simple. We talked a while, and I learned she liked to play golf. So did I. But I hadn't done too much of it since the babies came, because Mable didn't like it. She said it was too slow and boring a game; she wasn't old enough for it yet, and we hadn't started having individual hobbies as yet. Well, to get back to Eadie, before she lit her second cigarette, we were on our way out the door for the Green Ways Golf Course out at Meadowbrook. We only played nine holes. She was pretty good. She beat me.

I drove her home, and we made a date to play eighteen holes the following Wednesday afternoon.

That next week, I felt guilty, wondering if I should tell Mable about the golf. But she didn't even ask me what I had planned for my afternoon off—and when I said I'd probably stay at the office again, she just smiled and went on about her business. I guess this is what is called love and faith and trust and all those things, but to me it was being "taken for granted." At the garage door I couldn't help turning back and saying, "...that is, unless I find a cute babe to take to bed for half a day!" and she just said something about don't be so vulgar.

I didn't plan on doing anything wrong with Eadie, so help me. But I couldn't ignore her softness, her full high breasts that seemed to be constantly in my way when I got near her. And she had a little laugh that really got to me. She loved martinis, even in the middle of the day. I found this out when we had to wait to tee up. She could drink a couple and still play pretty good golf. She didn't say much about her past, except that her ex-husband was a golfer; they had won a couple of trophies as a team.

It got so that we spent every Wednesday afternoon together, and then I would find an excuse to go somewhere alone on Saturday or Sunday evenings, which would mean I'd go over to Eadie's apartment.

Then one Saturday night it happened. I was unfaithful to Mable. I went to bed with Eadie. *And she was teriffic!*

Mable had taken Billy and Benny over to her mothers for the weekend. She didn't ask me if I wanted to go along. She took it for granted I wouldn't like to go, maybe because I'd said other times I wish she didn't go over to Clayton so often to see her folks; it took so long getting there and her mother was such a dreary, complaining person—her father's jokes bored the hell out of me. So this weekend when she said she was going because her mother was in bed with a sprained something-or-other, she didn't ask me to go and I didn't offer. She had her own car and didn't mind driving.

I had a glorious weekend. Eadie and I went to the Greeks for a dinner that was out of this world. Then we went up to the Sky Room for cocktails and dancing. Then back to her apartment at two in the morning. I had kissed her before, lots of times. Not very passionate kisses, just nice kisses to thank her for being fun, for putting up with a married man who intended to stay married.

I didn't *plan* to do anything wrong that night. Sure I'd had dreams, some pretty nice ones, in which I had undressed her, held her—but this Saturday when we got home and she told me to fix a martini while she got into another dress, I got to thinking about how she must look in that other room, in her slip or whatever she had on that minute. So I went to the door she had left half open and I called her. She said, "Yes, Hal— what do you want?" and then she came to the door and I knew what I wanted. I guess she did too. Because she didn't protest when I took her in my arms and kissed her. Her skin was so smooth, so warm, I couldn't keep my hands off of her. She felt like velvet. I don't know where the words came from, but I was telling her I loved her, that she was wonderful, and she was saying the same things back to me. Then, before I realized what she was doing, she had me by the hand, taking me back into the bedroom. And I made love to her. She was as wonderful as I had dreamed she'd be.

Well, by the end of two months I was really floating on a cloud. I thought Eadie went for me in a big way. I started to wonder if I could swing it financially if I got a divorce and had to pay alimony to Mable to keep her in the house with the same setup we had now, and do the same somewhere else for Eadie—but it was just halfway daydreaming.

And all this time Mable never once asked me where I was at certain times when I wasn't home. She swallowed every lie I told her, hook, line and sinker. If she noticed I was occasionally short of money, she didn't question it. She was so sweet and loving when we were in bed that I would feel so guilty I would force myself to make love to her, which wasn't always easy after I'd been with Eadie for the same purpose.

Then we got this new district manager, Ed Boyer. He was a big, tall, rather good-looking guy, I guess, to women. I didn't think much of his type. In fact, I thought he was quite homely. He took over Brian's desk and handled all the big accounts. I hadn't noticed him talk more to Eadie than the other girls. He was one of those hale and hearty, always giving out with a belly laugh about everything type of guys. But she came up to me Tuesday night and said she couldn't go golfing the next day. She had something unexpected turn up. I tried not to act too disappointed. I didn't have any strings attached to her I kept reminding myself.

But that next morning I didn't do a lick of work. And when I saw her go out the door with this Boyer, I saw red. She should have told me, I thought. I went on home and sat around the house, wasting my afternoon off.

And I didn't have another date with Eadie. She smiled at me, talked to me in the office, but that was it. When I tried to pin her down to seeing me later, to let me talk to her, she would be in a rush—then this Boyer would come up and they would leave together. Of course everybody in the office knew they were going out on dates. She didn't have to be secretive with him like she had to be about me. He was single, about thirty-five, and they had no reason to hide their friendship I soon had to admit was a romance.

Then all of a sudden there was a collection for a wedding present—they were getting married and moving back to his old district.

I don't know how I got through those next days. I felt so lost, so empty, and so *cheated*. Mable was so sweet and understanding I practically barked at everything she said. She let me know that she thought I was coming down with something, or that I was working too hard. She made the kids tiptoe around and she wouldn't let them have the TV up high or play ball in the house. I thought I'd lose my mind, she showered me with so much love and kisses and consideration.

I'd sit there and think, you wouldn't be doing all this lovey-dovey stuff if you knew I cheated on you— that I took another woman to bed. You wouldn't snuggle up so close in my arms if you knew I had held Eadie Williams in them. And somehow *it got to bugging me that Mable didn't know*. That nobody knew. I got to wondering if Eadie ever told Ed Boyer that we had been sleeping sweethearts.

Then all of a sudden I got guilt-stricken. I got to making all kinds of promises to myself: that I would never step out again, that I would always be a faithful husband to my wonderful wife. And I couldn't keep from saying these things to Mable.

One Sunday we were sitting in the living room; the kids had just been bedded down and I got the notion to fix us a drink, a martini. I guess subconsciously I was washing away the remainder of my sins. I fixed the martinis, which Mable didn't care too much about until I told her I wanted to fix them for a sort of celebration.

"Celebration of what, sweetie," she asked me, and I went over and kissed her on the neck and said, "For having the most wonderful wife in the world."

"Well, thank you, Hal. It's been a while since you said anything like that. What brings this on?" she asked, holding my face against her a minute. "You keep acting like this and I'll go in and put on that new nightie I've been saving for vacation."

I told her to go ahead, put it on, and I kept insisting until she got up to do it. First she stopped to take the martini glass I had ready. I drank part of mine, then I gave a toast.

"To a man who finally realized what a dope he was," I said, and she took a sip then asked me what I meant.

"Well, any man's a dope who looks at another woman when he has a wife that's built like you are." And I meant it. I meant everything else I was saying. So help me, I really did love Mable. I thought she was really stacked while I stood there looking at her, and I kept talking. I kept saying a lot of things I wish I'd kept my damn big mouth shut about. Then, out of nowhere, the words were there. I was promising her I would never cheat on her again, never look at another woman again.

"Never do it *again*," she said, and something about the way she looked at me, I just couldn't believe I had so completely pulled the wool over her eyes all those weeks. I just couldn't believe she hadn't even guessed there was another woman. And something deep inside me couldn't just stand there and be quiet!

I had to tell her. I started with the golf game. And worked up to the weekend she went to her mother's. I got so carried away with my confession, with baring my soul, I didn't notice how pale and rigid she got, how tight her mouth became, until her eyes blazed and glared at me. All of a sudden she threw her glass at me, and martini ran down my face.

"You *bum*! You dirty, lying, stinking, cheating, no good *bum*!" she said in a tone I'd never heard before. I tried to get my arms around her.

"But it's all *over*, honey." I kept trying to kiss her, to hold her. "It was just one of those—things. I didn't love her. She was just—like I said—one of those *things* . . . ." but she pulled away.

"Don't you dare touch me!" she cried, and she hit out at me until I had to let her go. She didn't actually cry, but her eyes filled with tears and now her voice got quieter. "To think I've always trusted you, always thought you were the ideal husband, the perfect father," she said, each word slow and careful to cut into me like a razor-edged knife. "Well, you'll never get another chance to make a fool of me!" And before I knew what she was doing, she was in the bedroom pulling suitcases down from the shelf in the closet. *My* suitcases. I watched while she threw *my* clothes into them. Then she carried them out to the living room where I still stood, watching her, and she practically threw them at me, saying something about I could get out right then and there.

I was so stunned, I got out. I went out and walked until I saw a cab and had him take me down to the Drake Hotel.

That was a year ago. I thought at the time she would get over it. I kept calling her on the phone, begging her to listen to me, to believe me, but she divorced me. And the judge gave her practically everything she asked for! She got the house, the best of the cars, the furniture, plus alimony for her and support for the kids. At this rate, it's all I can do to have an occasional dinner date. I guess I could have fought it, made her lawyer come up with some *proof* of my infidelity—but I didn't. Smart ass that he was, he might just have gotten hold of Eadie and had her testify against me!

I'm telling my story to advise you other husbands. For chris' sake quit while you're ahead. Be smart, and don't be the dumb jerk I was. While I write this it's all I can do to keep from hitting myself in the head for being so dumb. Now when I have visiting rights with my boys I have the feeling they look at me as if I was some sort of monster that deserted them. I want to tell them I still love their mother, and it's really her fault we're not together because she won't give me another chance—but I can't find the right words to explain things to two little boys.

I don't care about money for this story, editor. I just want you to publish it so maybe other husbands will read it and know to be smart and keep their big mouths shut, not feel they have to confess everything to their wives.

This story could be made into a salable one with the following changes:

First, change golf to bowling, a less expensive sport for the middle class. Eliminate martinis, and make it wine or beer, or just a "drink." Let Mable go to her mother's on the bus (only one car in the family). Hal must "repent," be sorry he cheated on Mable, and vindicate himself. He must decide of his own will to quit Eadie. He must "mature," be strong, tell her he is finished with the affair and wants to be a good husband again. To further vindicate himself he perhaps tells Mable what he had done in a weak moment because he was left alone, and ask her forgiveness.

Now, for story inspirational quality, Mable tearfully forgives him. Both agree to put the affair out of their minds and, for the childrens' sake, make a special effort to pick up where they left off. The reader is left with the feeling that they will now find a lifetime of real happiness together.

Note, also, that in this story when Mable forgives Hal she is telling other wives who have gone through the same or a similar situation that a philandering husband need not permanently break up a marriage if both sincerely want to save it.

8

SPECIAL TECHNIQUES AND SOURCES

Often, in speaking before writing groups, listeners who have written confession stories that have not sold blame it on the supposition that confession magazines do not want "good writing." They feel slick-quality writing is rejected because it is over the heads of the reader. But in discussing this point with several of them, I found that their interpretation of "slick writing" was the use of obscure words which few readers would understand, and complicated sentences difficult to follow.

✳The true definition of "good writing" is selective writing. That is, you select words and phrases which say what you want to say, and which are within the possible educational advantages and comprehension of most potential readers. Words are supposed to create emotion; stimulate one or more of the five senses. They should make a reader feel, see scenes and places, and create emotional reaction to the events in the story. But if a reader has to look up every other word in the dictionary he has lost the impact of the plot and theme before he has read three pages.

In many ways, more discriminatory word choice is required to write a confession story than may be necessary in a so-called slick magazine story. The reason is largely that confession magazines buy on word-length basis. It takes better word selection to say what you want to say and expect the story to "reach" the reader when the length of the story is strictly limited. And to reach the reader with "participation" impact, the story must show a complete change in the main character's life, his philosophy, and/or in his approach to the future, to his family or loved ones, as well as to himself. Furthermore, because word length is specified by editors of confession magazines, the writer cannot waste too many of those words on long, detailed descriptions of the smell of rain, the glory of a sunset, the way the ocean roared that night on the beach with Tommy when it happened . . . .

For example, if you are doing a scene in which it is raining, you say simply:

> It was raining when I came out of the building. I didn't have an umbrella, otherwise I'd not have accepted David's offer to drive me home. I had promised myself never to be alone with him again, to subject myself to his infectuous charms; so when I got into the car and settled beside him I kept repeating over and over "I won't hear him—I won't listen to anything he says . . . ."

This scene tells the reader that something is going to happen *because* of the rain. That is the important point, not the smell or feel of it or how it shines on the pavement.

Let's consider for a moment two important elements in any story, even more important in the confession or personal experience story: Reality and Logic. ✓

To the characters who appear in your story, these have vital application. Reality contributes to conviction or believability of the character's behavior and reactions. Logic supports reality, or denies it. For example, almost everyone to some extent has a dual personality; that is, he is neither all good nor all bad. This applies to your "hero" character as well as to the "bad guy." Therefore, you emphasize more strongly the desirable and admirable qualities of your hero while "playing down" his shortcomings. And you reverse this treatment with the villain or bad guy. Do not try to balance or justify the good *and* bad in your hero; nor in reverse with your bad guy. Otherwise your reader is confused; isn't sure which character he wants to win. And sympathy for your main character, wanting him or her to win, is a vital element of any story.

Anyone who has ambitions to write, whether for money or for personal fulfillment, should do as much reading as possible. Read books that tell you about life, even if it is not the kind of life you live; read the classics if you did not read them in school; for many of these were, in a sense, confession stories, whether told in first person or third, because the emotional impact was much the same. Examples: *Little Women, Tale of Two Cities, Treasure Island*.

The reading of poetry—all kinds of poetry—is one of the best ways to learn word value. For poetry is, to a large degree, a story distilled to its very essence; the "perfume," so to speak, from a thousand crushed flowers. A confession story writer must know the true "essence" of words;

that is, learn to select a word which often can portray as much to the reader as a paragraph of descriptive phrases.

Poetry reading can serve also in the matter of story material. Suppose, for instance, you consider turning Edgar Allen Poe's famous poem *Annabelle Lee* into a fiction story dealing with contemporary problems and time. It might go something like this:

Your name is Mike Hansen. You are in love and want to marry a girl named Annabelle. But she has an incurable disease (perhaps a blood disease, to modernize the story) which she is unaware of, although her family knows about it. They know her life will be a short one, and they have told Mike about it to prevent his asking her to marry him. They have made it clear that she can never bear children because of the illness. But Mike loves Annabelle. He refuses to break off the relationship. Annabelle loves Mike and believes her family is being cruel to keep them apart. So against family opposition Mike and Annabelle elope. Mike has a good job and can afford to take care of medical bills if and when they come along.

Now for the problem: Annabelle wants a child. Mike knows that having a child, or trying to have one, will hasten her death, so without her knowledge he has a sterilization operation which is performed by a doctor who is aware of Annabelle's condition. But Annabelle continues to hope and pray for pregnancy. And now the results of Mike's "sin"—marrying the girl against her family's honest objection—begin to emerge. He suffers seeing his wife suffer. He must find a way to vindicate himself, and the writer must create a logical and effective solution to the problem he has created.

Any one of several solutions would be effective: Perhaps a new cure has been found for Annabelle's condition, and she will now be able to bear a child, but Mike cannot be the father of any child now. Or, Mike confesses to Annabelle what he had done and why, and they decide to adopt a child even if the doctors are right and she hasn't a long life ahead of her. But this particular story should not have a happy ending; some stories must end unhappily because that is the only true-to-life formula. However, an unhappy ending which is not logical or justified will sound contrived to the reader and the whole purpose of the story is lost. As pointed out earlier, every story must have a reason-for-being: to prove something. And almost all stories are, in a general sense, based on one of the old copybook maxims mothers and grandmothers have been reciting for a long time: Honesty is the best policy. More blessed to give than receive. A good deed is more to be desired than gold. And hundreds more such mottoes which most of us grew up with, and by which our standards of life were established. Out of these, literally hundreds of stories, each with individual characters and purpose, may be created by an imaginative writer. And unless there is some imaginative talent to start with, few writers succeed.

Saleable stories must be planned. We have touched on this earlier in this book, but it cannot be emphasized too frequently. If you think about it a moment you will realize that *everything* about you was made to a pattern: your typewriter, the table which holds it, the chair you sit in; the lamps and the carpet. The clothes you wear.

Making something to pattern means proportioning the material you have to work with whether it is cloth, wood, stone, or any other basic material. In every case, material is measured and cut or hewn to fit the design in the creator's mind, and to serve some definite purpose.

If you, as a writer, have one story you want to write primarily to "get if off your mind," then you have little need for sources of story material. You lived that one story, know the people involved, and having put it on paper whether you sell it or not, that's most likely an end to it.

On the other hand, if in writing that one story you are inspired to do more stories about the problems of friends and neighbors, or stories you "dream up," then it is well to have a plentiful source at hand. Sooner or later you will exhaust the quality of originality in your stories if you depend only on friends and neighbors; for their problems tend to fall into categories which are somewhat over-worked in fiction: divorce, the other woman (or man), child drug addiction, financial problems, all the elements that go into most families' lives.

Professional writers occasionally run into what they call a "dry period."

"I can't find anything worth writing about," one of my writer friends complained. "It's all been said before."

"Of course," I told her, "but not in the same way."

"What do you mean? Don't you ever run out of story ideas?"

I told her that of course I did; every writer does occasionally. "But I have a source of supply. The classics, the Bible, the daily newspaper; sometimes a single remark overheard from a passerby on the street starts my imagination working."

There is story material in almost everything around you. Knowing how to turn that material into a story is what this book is all about. Learn the basic rules for writing: planning, plotting, development of characters and situations, and the handling of human values. Then read and look about you. You'll find plenty of good story material which can be adapted to the writing of confession stories, even personal experience books.

The ability to learn to write is, to a large extent, born with you. However, if you have that instinct, that burning desire to write, and are willing to listen and study, you can be taught techniques, formula, patterns, plotting—the ingredients which make up a finished story or book. But no instructor should try to change your own individual style of writing. The instructor is helpful only if he or she helps you to follow the basic rules of writing. Basic rules are something like the stone foundation of a house. Once it is in place you can build many styles of houses upon it.

When you have had several stories published, you will begin to proportion and balance your material almost automatically. Some beginning writers find that reading a well-constructed magazine story, which is somewhat in the category of the one they are planning to write, helps to "put them in rhythm"; that is, to pick up the flow of language and subconsciously feel the pace of the story they want to emerge.

The average short story of five to six thousand words has eight to eleven major scenes divided among the major elements of the story. The following will give you a workable breakdown of scenes:

Scene No. 1 In this you introduce conflict, most of the major elements, and all of the factors that weigh against your central story character. The result of these pressures activated against him will force him later to make a "destiny decision."

Scene No. 2 This is usually a "flashback scene" and tells the reader those things he should know about your main character: his background, perhaps childhood; the reason he is now behaving as he does; gives his attitude toward some person, thing, or conflict *before* the story happened. This scene prepares the reader for what the character does later, so it will not be a complete surprise or shock. (This can be used as a "parallel" scene.)

Scene No. 3 This is called the "destiny decision scene." In this area of story, your main character commits himself to a plan of action. He makes up his mind to do something about the trouble he is in. The physical visible direction of the plot changes when he makes his decision. (Do not confuse this scene with the "obligatory scene.") You show how much he has to lose by this decision he makes.

Every scene must show a change, or potential for a change, of your central character's attitude toward the main problem upon which your story is built. This change can be either progress or regression. Do not switch back and forth in every scene. Do not have your character first a good guy, then a bad guy. Make up your mind before you start to write the story how you want him to be at the end, and work toward that goal in every scene, a little at a time.

Scene Nos. 4, 5, and 6 These are called "obstacle scenes" and may be thought of as "conflict" scenes, because this area of the story gives the reader all the setbacks, the hazards, the *obstacles*, your main character faces after he makes his "destiny decision." Each one of these obstacle scenes should bring your hero just a little closer to his goal, to an answer to his problem, to *a solution for his problem.*

Scene No. 7 This is the "ramp arena scene," the all-important scene. It is also called the "obligatory scene." Your central character (hero or heroine) enters this scene with all odds against him. This is the biggest, most important scene in the story.

Up to this point, you have shown in visible drama two philosophies in conflict. *Outward* conflict as well as *inner* conflict within the character. (He has been battling the way of the criminal *versus* the law; success *versus* failure; love *versus* hate, etc.) Now he *obligates* himself to a future way of life by another final decision. This scene proves your point. It exploits your main theme; gives the answer to the story problem.

Throughout your story you have, up to this scene, shown a gradual potential for your character to change from being a bum, a cheat, an alcoholic, a thief, etc. In this area of story, the "obligatory scene" area, *the change is completed.* The way you show him now to the reader is the way the reader believes he will be the rest of his life.

There are six basic points to the "obligatory scene":

1. Two choices are offered the main character in the form of two specifics. One representing Philosophy Y, one Philosophy Z. (There are always two philosophies in every story—one that wins, one that loses; one for and one against the story problem solution.)

2. There is a moment of inner doubt, inner agony, that interim before he "throws the fight," "breaks the safe," "rapes the girl," "tells on his wife," "decides to

have the abortion." That one small bit of time he hangs on the fence trying to decide what he is going to do.

3. In this "obligatory scene," you exert your theme vehicle. (Remember this is the person or thing that influences, but never battles, your main character— a word, a deed, a thought, a person; even a memory can be used.)

4. Plainly exploit for the reader the central character's inner philosophy, his philosophic decision.

5. Translate that decision in the visible, onstage act.

6. The result, meaning the perimeter of the theme, problem and solution.

To repeat, all of the above six areas are covered in the one big dramatic scene of your story, the "obligatory scene."

Scene No. 8 This is the "conclusion" scene. It ends the story, ties up all the loose ends, more or less summarizes the theme for the reader. This is usually a short scene.

Additional scenes can be minor ones, stepping stones to the obstacles scenes; sometimes given as inner conflict scenes.

Some stories develop to the best advantage if opened at the climax, or with the "obligatory" scene. The major portion of the story is then handled as "flashback," and comes back up to the point of opening. Be certain to return to the opening scene when you finish with the flashback area. Do not tell the reader too much in the portion of the "obligatory" scene that you use. Keep him guessing; make him have to read the entire story.

Regardless of what scene you use to open or begin your story, the story problem should come through to the reader in the first 300 words; definitely no later than 500. At this point the editor (and reader) should know whether it is a story about a love triangle; an unfaithful wife or husband; premarital sex; dope addiction; family strife because of a mother-in-law; financial troubles; delinquent teenager; etc. The viewpoint, male or female, should be known immediately.

By the end of the first 1,000 words or four-and-one-half pages of a twenty page story (which would be about 5,000 words total), all of your characters should have been introduced, or at least mentioned, even though they come into the onstage conflict later.

At this time, the locale should be established, as well as the time (i.e., the season of the year), the age and social level of the story characters, etc.

In summation: If you have trouble getting started with a story, start to write the conclusion, or any one of the eight major scenes. This often helps a writer get into the feel of the problem. Later, you can work this first writing into the area in which it belongs. After a story is finished, many writers then rearrange the scenes. The only extra work involved is the changing of verb tenses and some cutting.

Do not be afraid to use the red pencil on your finished story. Cut out all of the extra scenes you threw in, scenes that have no basic purpose for being in the story.

9

WOMEN WRITERS VS MALE VIEWPOINT

The male-viewpoint confession story by a woman writer deserves some special attention.

If you are a woman writer, the chances are you tend to let your male characters think the way you would in a given situation or set of circumstances. The best way to avoid this error is literally to put yourself in the man's place. Try to imagine how he would feel or react. Actually it might be exactly opposite to what you or any woman would feel or say in a similar situation. For instance, a woman might "gush" over something that excited or pleased her; a man would be more reserved. In tense situations, a woman usually expresses emotion in one way or another—cries out, gets hysterical, or perhaps resorts to tears for nervous relief. A man would likely "clam up," or curse; or in a fight let action speak for him; or in a quarrel with wife or girlfriend likely would get sarcastic or bluntly tell the other person off and walk away.

Conflict between the sexes is the basis for most stories to one degree or another. In marriage, when husband and wife are always in accord and everything goes peaceably from day to day with no disagreements, no difference of opinions, things are pretty sure to become dull and uninteresting. The man starts looking for excitement outside, the woman to flirt with the milkman.

The same rules in general apply to stories. A story is, after all, designed to deliver suspense, excitement, emotional reaction of some kind or it isn't a story, it is a list of names and events. What pleasure would you get out of reading a story in which you knew exactly what was going to happen before it happened? Events must not be predictable, even emotional reactions; but neither should they be so twisted about as to make the story unconvincing.

On the other hand, a story that "ties everything up in pink ribbons" is pretty sure to be a dull story.

If you are a woman and the story you want to tell is best told from the male viewpoint, it would be a good idea to spend some time on "research." I don't mean the library kind of research. I do mean listening and observing with a purpose; not the "in one ear and out the other" kind of listening. Really hear the way men express themselves in a variety of circumstances. This shouldn't be difficult. Any place men and women gather is your research place—church, PTA meeting, at the office if you are a working woman or girl, in lunch rooms, on buses or other kinds of transportation vehicles. Listen and record for later use in stories.

Here are a couple of examples of published stories to illustrate the rules mentioned above:

Nervously I paced the corridor outside the labor room and hoped everything was okay. It seemed like hours since they'd taken Mary inside. A few minutes later the door opened and Dr. Bowens and a nurse came out. I could tell by their expressions that something was wrong.

"Sorry, Ray, but there's no easy way to tell you this. You're going to have to make one of the hardest decisions in your life—and you're going to have to do it now."

I asked him what he meant and in a few short nonmedical terms he explained that I had to choose whose life I wanted to save—my wife's or my unborn child's—because it wasn't possible for both of them to live.

"Are you crazy? I don't want a choice. I want them both! I'm not going to play God, deciding who to let live and who to let die. Mary and I both want the baby. And I want Mary!" We'd only been married a little over a year, but it was long enough to know I couldn't live without her.

"I'm sorry, Ray. There's no other way. You have to decide."

"How can there possibly be a choice? Of course you've got to save Mary. What good's the kid with no mother? And what would Jody do?" And what would

I do without Mary? She was everything in the world to me. "I don't want my wife to die! Why did you wait this long to tell me there was a possibility of . . . of . . . ." I couldn't say it.

"She's getting the best medical help available, Ray. We're doing everything possible." Dr. Bowens put his hand on my shoulder, as if to stop the tremble of anger and fear that shook me. "Perhaps if we get a little extra help from the Man up there, who knows? Why not sit down over there and think about it a minute? Let the Lord help you to decide."

"That's one way to pass the buck!" I said. "You want to blame it either on me or God if anything goes wrong. Why don't you doctors see that such decisions don't have to be made? What is this—a church or a hospital?"

"There's very little difference sometimes," he answered, and the tone of his voice made me ashamed I'd blown up.

In this story, the mother and baby both lived. This is shown in the summary, after the obligatory scene, and is the area of the story in which Ray "matures," grows up in his thinking; changes his earlier philosophy about God and religion. When the story is brought back onstage after the flashback scene, Ray is still in the hospital "sweating it out." His nine-year-old stepson joins him. It is in this scene with little Jody that Ray understands for the first time what strength is possible through faith.

Then comes the *summary*, which is a brief focusing on the lessons learned through the events of the story, and leaves the reader with a satisfactory feeling. You want your reader to be inspired by your conclusion. Be careful, however, not to get too emotional or wordy.

Just then Dr. Bowens came up behind the nurse. He pulled off his mask. "Congratulations, father. Pretty little girl you've got in there. We'll have her cleaned up and weighed in a minute."

"Mary . . . ?" My mouth was so dry I couldn't get my question out.

"Fine. She's still asleep. Be out for another hour or so, but you can go in for a minute if you're quiet."

Mary didn't know I was in the room. I stood there beside the bed and had the oddest feeling I was seeing her for the first time. I never before realized she was so beautiful. Suddenly she wasn't just a woman. She was everything missing in my life as a child, as a young man. She was that "other love," the one it takes to know complete happiness. The love it took a nine-year-old boy to tell me was spelled F-A-I-T-H. I closed my eyes a moment and I said, "Thank You."

Then Mary woke up. "Honey?"

My heart was so full all I could do was lean down and put my cheek against hers and whisper, "I love you so much!" I would wait until she was fully awake to let her know I was the luckiest, the richest man in the world.

Amy Joy is a year old. This week we're going to buy extra camping gear to fit her needs because it's fishing time again and I found out there's a small church not a stone's throw from the lake. I told Mary there wouldn't be any music and no one would be very dressed up and I understand they depend on visiting or voluntary preachers, but she agreed it will suit us fine.

"Sleeping Bag Party" was the story of a high school boy who wanted to be accepted by the "in" crowd. He thought the girl he was to take to the cabin party would expect him to know all about love and sex, which he didn't; he knew almost nothing about it. The conclusion was to prove to the readers (other young boys and girls) that there is nothing disgraceful with a boy being as virtuous as a girl. In the "obligatory" scene, where Joe matures in his thinking, he discovers that Millie, his date, is just as inexperienced in such matters as he is, and she intends to stay that way until she is married. The obstacle scenes include a dramatized one in which the cabin catches on fire while they are all in their sleeping bags—all but Joe and Millie, who are down at the river bank to keep from having to share a sleeping bag the way the others were doing. The opening lets the reader know at once it is a teenage boy's story:

> I'd been trying since I entered Stetson High in January to get into the High Flier's bunch, and all of a sudden there I was—in.
> It wasn't that I particularly cared much about the five guys themselves or that they were kids of the important folks in Canton, but Red Wade, the leader of the gang, went steady with Myrtle Brian, and I was crazy about Myrtle's cousin Millie, who lived with her. These kids always went around and did everything

together. So to get anywhere with Millie, I had to be part of the gang.

It got so I dreamed about her at night; got all cold-and-hot feeling at the same time when I'd see her in the halls at school, and when she talked or smiled at me, I was a complete blank the rest of the day. But so far, I couldn't tell if she liked me or not. The only thing in my favor was that she didn't pay attention to any other boy in school.

This Thursday we were all sitting in a booth at the White Dot, where a lot of kids hung out.

Since I was still an "outsider," I sat on a chair at the end of the booth table, but it was okay because Millie was beside me. I was trying not to be so conscious of her closeness so I could follow what Ruby was saying.

"It's a perfect setup," Ruby repeated, going over again the bit about us all going to her uncle's cabin at Canyon Lake for the weekend. "You can use the same excuses we did for the Christmas-week party, and it'll be just as swell a shindig—if you remember!" she added, and the others made knowing smiles and chuckles, all but me, because I wasn't at that party.

"Sounds real cool, man, real cool," Red Wade tightened his arm around Myrtle's shoulder. "The back seat of that tin lizzy's been cramping my style lately," he said, loud enough for the rest of us to hear. I pretended not to be embarrassed, but I was.

"Well, Joe, this is where we separate the men from the boys," Curt Weldon said to me. "You go on this party and you're officially one of us, right you guys?"

He looked around at the others and they all gave me the okay sign.

I nodded toward Millie, who was fiddling with her purse. "Sure, I want to go," I said quickly, "if—if Millie goes."

"Where I go, Millie goes," Myrtle declared.

Her cousin looked at me a second with a sort of half smile, then said "Why not? Sounds like a blast." Then she added something about putting money in the juke, and she got up.

Note that this opening sets up the problem. These high school kids are planning a big "blast" without letting their parents know the truth. (Dope was not a problem in the high schools when this story was written. The big problem then among teenagers was promiscuous sex.) The "summary" winds up the story for the reader after the problem is solved:

Red helped me pull the burned sleeping bag toward the door. Then a truck rolled in front and turned its lights on us. Everybody was standing on the porch but Ruby, who was in the burned zipped-up bag. The place cracked and roared while it burned. In just a second we were forced into the yard.

Mr. Bowan was the man in the truck. He'd seen the smoke and called the fire department before he started over. But by the time the volunteer truck got there, about all that was left was the stone fireplace. Nobody had much on but me and Millie. We rolled the cars into a gully because the keys were in burned-up pants pockets.

Mr. Bowan worked on Ruby to get the smoke out of her lungs. I got sick to my stomach when I saw her blistered face and her hair—rather, her burned scalp. The hair was all gone. I guess she'll be a mess for a long time, and she'll probably always have scars.

That next week was pretty bad for all us kids with our parents, and we were all worried about whether or not Ruby would pull through. She did, thank heaven.

I know it was my fault and Millie's, too, I guess, as much as anybody's, because nobody held a gun to us to make us go. Anyway, Millie is still my girl, and we're going to get married soon as I graduate and get a full-time job. Millie wants to just move in with us and help Grandma with the kids until we start having some of our own. And considering the way I love Millie, we'll probably have a houseful.

The *second theme* in this story, which was almost as important as the first, was that teenagers are prone to trouble when they deliberately do things they know their parents do not approve of. For example, having a boy-and-girl unchaperoned weekend party at Ruby's uncle's cabin.

Another example is "I Wanted a Wife Not a Baby Machine." This was published in *True Experiences* magazine. It is the story of a young husband who does not want children. He remembers too vividly his childhood when there were always too many mouths to feed. When his wife, Gloria, becomes pregnant, she is afraid to tell him, knowing how he feels about children. Finally she decides to have an abortion, which seems a better way out than facing his anger and possible resentment of the child later on.

The obligatory scene takes place when Bruce finds out that his wife has gone to an abortionist. Now he is more worried about something happening to her to endanger her life than whether or not they can afford a child. The reader realizes he isn't a pinch-penny or a brute, but really a good and gentle man in love with his wife, and that he never would have permitted her to go through such an ordeal as an abortion. The theme—the point to be proved by the story—is that there is less "sin" in being pregnant than in taking the selfish way out; that a young couple should be able to afford one or two children if their marriage is to have meaning and purpose. Another theme this story proves is that young husbands, who have lived an improverished childhood, understandably have a fear of not being able to care for their own children properly; but when the wife becomes pregnant they are usually more enthusiastic about the event than more affluent young husbands.

Note that from the first line the reader is informed that this is to be a male-viewpoint story:

"You think you're pregnant?" I said, looking over Mom's note at my wife Gloria. She hadn't touched her coffee. "Well, you better think again, honey, and think yourself unpregnant," I said, chuckling. "Remember our agreement—no kids." A minute ago Gloria had said she was getting so nauseous at the smell of food and driving in the car that she'd better get some carsick pills from Dr. Ford before we took off on our trip. I told her I'd stop at the drugstore for some pills, then added, "Now how about it? Think you can take off Monday? That'll give us three days."

All Mom's note had said was, "Son, your Pop's sick and he asked about you. Come if you can." I realized the idea of driving 300 miles to my folks' old farm in Rosedale was about as unpleasant an idea to Gloria as it was to me. I hadn't been home in five years and my family had never met my wife.

"I'll bet Pop doesn't even remember my name. Probably he got to counting heads and just found one was missing," I laughed. But the memories that suddenly crowded back weren't funny. I was the oldest of ten children—five sisters and four brothers.

"There's no crime in being pregnant, Bruce," Gloria said. "We *are* married, you know—four years the eighteenth of this month. We've got about everything we need, and no bills to pay, and . . . ."

I stopped her. "Look, honey, four years or forty years—what's the difference? I want a wife, not a baby machine!" I gulped the last of my coffee and bent over to kiss her goodbye before leaving for work. "There's your answer," I said, tapping Mom's note. "I probably won't recognize my mother when I see her. I never knew her any way but pregnant, worn-out, overworked and underfed—and that's not going to be my wife's story, you can bet on that!"

"We don't need a dozen, honey. Just one or two." Her eyes were red, as if she were about to come down with a cold.

"Gloria, you don't look too hot. Maybe you're coming down with something. Why not take off this afternoon? Get things packed so we can leave early." I started again for the door but she stood in my way.

"Take a full day and a half off from work? You're actually suggesting I not only take off Monday, but this afternoon, too, and lose all that pay?" She didn't sound like my usual quiet, good-natured wife. "We'll both work, save money, have fun, go places, take terrific vacations, no babies to tie us down—you said!" she suddenly shouted accusingly.

I stood there listening, trying to figure out what the devil was wrong with her. She went on, "But where have we gone in four years but a couple of movies, a few picnics with Ralph and Liz? And I think the only reason you don't want any children is because they cost a few bucks. What's the point in being married?"

"There's the best argument for how I feel!" I pointed again to Mom's letter on the table. "Written on a scrap of paper from one of the kids' school tablets. You can bet if Pop dies either the County buries him or I do!" Once the words started I couldn't stop. "The first years he and Mom could have lived pretty nice off the farm's income, but every time he turned around there was another kid to clothe and feed. My old man couldn't even buy a fishing license to take us kids fishing, yet that was the only thing he could afford to do!"

"Did it ever occur to you that maybe your mother liked being pregnant, and didn't mind being poor?"

Gloria said. "That maybe your father wanted a big family? Did you ever think of that?"

I didn't think I'd heard right. "You serious? No one's that crazy! Especially not me!" Then, before I opened the door, I stopped and looked at her and I don't know why I said what I did. Ordinarily I'd have cut off my arm before I purposely hurt Gloria. But I added, "And any time you get lonesome for the patter of little feet, just stop by St. Mary's and remember why you were there!" I left without kissing her goodbye.

When your married couples are arguing, or fighting, make certain you know where to draw the line. Do not have them say or do things in anger that cannot be smoothed over later. If you let the husband or the wife say mean things, make certain you let the reader know this is unusual behavior. The reader must remain in *sympathy* with the characters, provided they are to *stay married and in love* in the story's conclusion.

Of course in my story Gloria does not have the abortion. She had decided not to go through with it about the same time Bruce learned where she had gone, and was realizing how wrong he'd been; that he still loved Gloria and wanted their child. They will find a way to handle the expense and now he knows that a child is worth the sacrifices parents often have to make.

Usually, resorting to accidents to provide a solution to a story problem is not good plotting, but in this case a minor accident was necessary in order to bring a legitimate doctor into the situation. Note that this was modified by the accident being little more than a "brush"; in other words, a device to create a needed event or incident for plot purposes. Such creative devices are acceptable if you make sure to make them logical and convincing, an integral part of the story action.

When both the main characters have come to realize their mistakes and the reader knows their love is strong enough to sustain a marriage with children, you need only a finishing paragraph along this line:

> She reached up and wiped the tears from my face, tears I wasn't at all ashamed of. "I do love you, Bruce. That's why I wanted a baby—to show the world how much I love you, like it was with your Ma. And I wanted you to give me something I could keep, call my own, not have to give away."

[Note: In St. Mary's orphanage, Gloria was never permitted to keep anything for herself, as her own— everything in the way of clothes or toys had to be shared.]

> Dr. Ford opened the door about then and hurried into the room. When he saw us both, he sighed with relief. "Well, nobody's dying around here, thank heavens," he said. "Now, just what's wrong? All I could understand on the phone was get here immediately."
>
> While he opened the little black bag, I explained about not seeing Gloria in the driveway, knocking her down. "She's pregnant, Doctor," I added. "Do you

think it hurt our baby any?" It seemed the most natural thing in the world to say "our baby."

Dr. Ford put his stethoscope to Gloria's chest and listened a second before he answered me. "There's something almost indestructible about healthy young mothers, Bruce. And love-babies are almost certain to stick it out to the finish line. Looks like a skinned leg's about it. Probably be a little stiff and sore tomorrow."

Dr. Ford was right. Our "love-baby," Bruce, Jr., stuck it out to the finish line. That was fourteen months ago. Now we're waiting for the girl, due in five months. And I think that'll about be it—unless, of course, it's another boy. Then we'll have to try again for the girl. Anyway, we'll go along with whatever the Planned Parenthood clinic says to do. For what we want most of all is to have as many kids as we can afford, but never to bring into the world any that are unwanted, unloved, or a burden.

And while I write this and look over at Gloria in her maternity smock, I believe I know how Pop must have felt each time he knew another kid was on the way. He probably hoped it was healthy and looked like its Ma. Then he knew he could love and want it all the more!

Compare the above sections of male-viewpoint stories with the ones offered in the female viewpoint to note the difference in tone.

These stories were all under 6,000 words.

10

PREPARING
MANUSCRIPT FOR MARKET

The presentation of a story is often as important as most ingredients of the story itself. Appearance in most things makes a difference. If you dress carelessly you will be accepted as a careless, shiftless person. If you present a well-groomed self to the public, you are likely to be respected and admired.

How much more important it is, then, to make sure your manuscript is "well-groomed" when sending it to an editor! Uniformity of presentation, in this case, is the objective. Consequently, general rules are accepted by publishers of both magazines and books. These make reading your story easier for an editor and labels you, in his opinion, a writer worth reading.

Here are those basic rules:

Always have your manuscript typewritten (handwriting is too difficult to read), and make sure the lines are double-spaced for faster reading. Use white paper, heavy enough to stand up under several readings and handling— 16-lb. to 20-lb. with some rag content is most desirable, with page size eight-and-one-half by eleven inches.

Margins should be as follows: approximately two inches from the top, one inch from the bottom; left margin one-and-a-half inches, right margin one inch.

Number pages either at the center top or right corner. Type your name in the upper left corner. Begin the *first* page only of the manuscript with a deep upper margin, about three inches, and type here the title of the story and the author's name. Drop down about four lines and let the story begin. Margins on all other pages are standard as indicated.

A title page will give your manuscript an organized appearance. On it place, in the center of the page, the title in all capital letters. Drop down two line spaces for the word "by"; then two more line spaces and type your name (the author). At the lower left hand, near the bottom of the page, type your full name and address, and be sure to add the zip number.

Manuscripts should be typed in regular pica-size type, which is a little larger than the type used for correspondence, and is easier for an editor to read. Use black typewriter ribbon; never use anything fancy such as bright blue or brown; these are harder on the eyes than black.

Make sure the manuscript is free from misspelled words, words that have been over-struck, etc. While a single word correction written in ink is forgiveable, whole lines and phrases definitely are not. These are like "patches" on your son's best pants! Be sure to enclose with the manuscript a self-addressed and stamped envelope for the return of your story in case the editor finds it unsuitable. If he or she buys it, the lost postage is a small item.

Never fold a manuscript. Mail it in a manila manuscript envelope, nine by twelve inches in size with a cardboard backing to prevent the postman from folding it.

Enclose with the manuscript a short note to the editor. Try to learn the fiction editor's name and use it. If you don't know it and can't find out what it is, then use simply, "The Editor," and a salutation of "Dear Editor." Such a note should be simple, something like: "I hope you will like my story (title). Thank you for considering it. Sincerely, (Jane Doe)"

Do *not* write long letters to the editor about how you came to write the story and that it really is a true story. Make sure you have a carbon copy of your story; things do get lost in the mails sometimes! Besides, if an editor should want a change on a page or two and wrote to you, referring to those pages, how would you know what she was talking about without a carbon?

Above all, do *not* pester an editor about your story if you don't hear in a week or two. Editors get hundreds of manuscripts every day; it takes time to consider each one.

The old proverb, "A watched pot never boils," is applicable here, too. Don't haunt the post office or mail box, and above all, don't talk about the story to friends and neighbors, even members of your family. If your story is purchased, it will be a nice surprise for everyone; if it is rejected you won't have to eat crow!

Not all stories by beginning writers are bought on first submittal, although this can, and does, happen. In case this doesn't happen with your story, don't be discouraged; editors have various reasons for rejecting a story, sometimes because they happen to have another story dealing with the same theme, or too many female viewpoint stories, or vice-versa. Select another magazine which you feel might be interested and submit it again. Again and again and again, if necessary. But too many rejections should tell you there is something wrong with the story.

Try to find out why it was rejected and correct the matter. Often that terific lead story in *xyz magazine* had been rejected several times before it found a "home" with another top-quality magazine because it was what *that* particular editor was looking for. This is true with the confession magazine market also. A story one editor does not need at the time may be exactly what another editor is looking for.

Manuscripts today may be sent by a special postage rate: *Special Fourth Class Rate.* Write that on the manila envelope addressed to the editor in which you enclose your manuscript. Under that designation write in parentheses: "Manuscript." This postal rate was devised for writers and publishers since first-class postage today would be prohibitive for many aspiring writers; and publishers receive hundreds of manuscripts (books and short stories) every day which have to be returned to senders who did not enclose return postage. That can add up to quite an item!

In the event your manuscript isn't bought on first or even the fifth submittal, and you still think it is worth further submittal, don't send it out again if it is "dog-eared." Retype it. A manuscript with a worn-out look isn't likely to receive a warm welcome on an editorial desk.

Most confession magazines have established a preferred average length for short stories of 5,000 words. With some markets this is the maximum length; with others it is average, in which case the story may run 6,000 words. A few markets set no limits on length, although it is logical to assume they want short story or novelette length material. Novelettes may run from 7,500 to 10,000 words. However, the most frequently purchased novelettes average around 7,000 to 8,000 words. Earlier, we pointed out the importance of not "padding" your stories; that is, making them longer by using more words than they warrant for proper telling.

Several market guide books are available to the beginning writer. In these, various kinds of markets are listed by category, giving the vital information such as names of editors, kinds of material sought, length desired or required, etc. The most prominent of these are: *The Literary Market Place, The Writers' Market,* and *The Writer.*

11

RACIAL CONSIDERATIONS

The color of a writer's skin has no real bearing on the kinds of stories he or she writes. If you are black and have stories dealing with white people which you feel are worth writing, there is no reason for not doing so. Stories deal with people of all races and color and creeds. All people have problems of one kind or another; and these problems are much the same whatever the color of their skin. Heartache plays no favorites. Neither do tears, worries, fears, unfaithfulness, jealousy, love, selfishness, or a hundred other emotional experiences which affect all mankind in various ways.

However there are a few special rules which should apply when writing about problems which concern characters of mixed race lines. For instance, if you are a black writer do not feel that you must let your black characters win out; be right all the time. If the story theme is one in which the black characters deserve to win out, then let them win; and the same applies to white characters. If a black man and a white man have good reasons to be adversaries, then let them be; let them resolve the problem which made them adversaries in the first place, but not on the assumption that one is superior (or inferior) to the other by reason of the color of his skin. The rules laid down by Moses in the Ten Commandments were for all mankind, whatever race or religion. Most problems stem from breaking those Commandments as we have indicated earlier.

Some story themes may depend upon a strictly racial problem. Such was the case in my story "I Didn't Know I Was a Negro" which was published in *Tan* magazine. The theme (the point to be proved) was that it should not be the ultimate goal of light-skinned Negroes to "pass" as white in order to find happiness or fulfillment. The plot concerned a Negro girl named Rose whose skin and hair are very light, and who is unaware that she is of the Negro race. A well-meaning aunt, thinking her niece will fare better in a white man's world, sends her north to a boarding school for white girls. For a while all seems to go well, then Rose falls in love and becomes engaged to a white boy. Only then she learns the truth and must "grow up," make a bitter and difficult choice. Ultimately she decides that being true to herself is most important; that she prefers to be a part of the Negro world to which she was born; that no happiness ever can come from denying one's birthright. Rose finds happiness and fulfillment working with her uncle who is a doctor at a hospital for underprivileged children.

Another story, also published in *Tan,* was titled "I Lived a Nightmare." This story, however, could have been published in any general magazine. It dealt with the situation of a stepfather who is a child molester. In my story the characters happened to be black only because the people on whom my story was based happened to be black. The "problem" could have happened to any mother, white or black, who marries a second time without knowing enough about the man who is to become stepfather to her daughter. Unfortunately this sordid problem does exist in many families, whatever race or color.

"We Were Parents of a White Child," was written especially for *Tan* and published by them. Yet it, too, could have been published in any confession magazine. The theme for the story came from my having read or listened to discussions about white couples who have a black child because of black ancestry of mother or father. Undoubtedly black couples could face the same problem in producing a white child. The story set out to prove that where love is strong enough the color of the child's skin never becomes a problem which cannot be solved.

Since this story illustrates the kind of special handling inter-racial stories may require, it is reproduced here for special study:

The opening of the story introduces the problem:

Perhaps no one cares about my own personal story, but because there may be others like me, I'm going to write it. Maybe someone will at least read it and understand the hell I've lived through before I came to accept the path God meant for me to take—and too, this will be like publicly apologizing to God for damning His ways, for cursing His power of birth, for doubting His reasons to subject a young girl to the misery, the confusion, the heartache I have known.

Until this past February 7th, a Friday, the world was just a wonderful normal place for a girl of eighteen in love to be a part of.

I changed buses twice to get over to Dover Place, then I had to walk three more blocks to find the address Mrs. Barnes, the director of my boarding school, had given me. The oddest feeling came over me while I hurried up the path to the huge old stucco house of 4817 Dover Place: an ominous kind of feeling that I should turn back now before it was too late, mixed with an overwhelming urgency and curiosity to see beyond the heavy oak door.

Vague, fuzzy memories crowded into my mind as if I had been here before, either long, long ago or in a dream. It was dark now, yet I knew exactly what the brass door knocker looked like before I reached it; I could see a little girl who had just come from a long, lonely bus ride stare up at the brass lion's head that looked like pure gold as the rays from the setting sun hit it at that other time.

A neat, middle-aged colored woman opened the door to me.

"Is this Mrs. Jefferson's house? Lenora Jefferson? I'm her niece, Rose, from the Elms Boarding School," I said, expecting her to invite me in. But she just stood there and looked at me so hard I felt uncomfortable.

"I didn't know I had an aunt until this afternoon," I went on, groping for words. "Are you the housekeeper? Mrs. Barnes said it was all right for me to come over—to see if my aunt had made any plans for me before she died . . . ."

"Hey Mom, shut the door. It's making a draft!" someone called out from inside, and for a moment I thought the woman intended closing the door in my face. A man came up behind her then and the dim light from the hall made his face so dark I couldn't tell if he was young or old.

"What's the matter, Mom? Who's she looking for?"

"This is your cousin Rose. You know, the girl your Aunt Lottie sent to school."

The name Aunt Lottie had a faintly familiar note, but I smiled and started to apologize for making a mistake. This man and woman were colored, and *his* Aunt Lottie couldn't possibly be mine. I looked at the address in my hand, a hand that was as white as this paper, as white as everyone I lived with at the Elms. "Is there an east and west Dover Place?"

"You have the right place, Rose. Come in," the woman said, and held the door wider.

I glanced up again at the brass knocker and a chill crept all through me, trying to remember the night when I was five years old and a woman, an Aunt Lottie, had brought me here from the bus station to stay one night before she took me in a cab to the big school in the country. I couldn't remember what the woman had looked like—*but surely she was white!*

I don't remember those next few minutes, but there I was inside a room of colored folks all sitting, staring and looking as uncomfortable as I felt. Then everyone talked at once. "Sit down, Rose," the woman who had answered the door said. "I'm your Aunt Ellie, Lenora's sister. This here's my boy, Joe. Your Uncle Ben, your cousin Clara and her husband-to-be, Hank, and Hank's brother—Dr. Wilbur Davis. He's an interne over at Mercy City Hospital."

Wilbur Davis stood up and held his hand out to me.

"Glad to know you, Rose," he said but I ignored him. I couldn't bear to look at any of them. I sat down on the nearest thing, the piano bench, and tried to believe the crazy, impossible things I had just heard—that these people belonged to me—they were my kin—*I was one of them.* They were all as dark as coffee beans!

I had taken it for granted all these years I was an orphan because Mrs. Barnes told me I was as far back as I could remember anything. And she believed it, too. I know she did—until she received the letter from the bank and called me into her office this afternoon to show it to me. The bank man wrote that my "bene-factress," an aunt, Mrs. Lenora Jefferson of this Dover Place address, had died a week ago and left no further provision for my school tuition so the Elms shouldn't expect any more checks.

Mrs. Barnes went on about how odd some people were, keeping themselves hidden from their relatives. But it didn't matter about the money. I was graduating in four months and getting married. They had a fund for the cap and gown rental, but I was so excited I practically grabbed the letter out of her hand.

"Gosh, Mrs. Barnes, if I had an aunt maybe I've got an uncle or cousins or grandparents. I want to go out there and see—right now! Bob can drive in to pick me up. If I've got any relatives I want him to meet them. He'll be as thrilled as I am." I was at the office door by the time it was all said and Mrs. Barnes just laughed.

"All right, Rose, go on. I don't blame you. I'll call Bob." Then she added, "But don't be too disappointed. I'm sure she was just an eccentric old spinster with a feeling of duty—maybe a promise she made your parents."

Despite what Mrs. Barnes said, all the ride out here I'd visualized inviting a bunch of Jeffersons to my graduation and then to Bob's and my wedding; of having an honest-to-goodness relative "stand up" for me; but I didn't want any part of *parany part of* this roomful of liars!

I didn't rave, scream or faint. I just sat there on that hard piano bench and listened to these strangers talk about me—listened and watched as if they were characters in a play.

About 750 words followed which covered Rose's visit with her new-found relatives, and her calling Bob not to pick her up. Then I used flashback to let the reader know what Rose's childhood was like before she was sent out into the "white man's world."

As if it were right outside the bus window, I saw that old shack with wads of newspapers and old catalogues nailed at the glassless windows to keep out the cold in winter months. Some days we were allowed to take the catalogues down for us kids to look at. I could almost smell the sweet pine needles in the burlap-covered mattress we slept on under the big Banyan tree in the back yard on hot summer nights—a mattress that was always crowded with warm squirming children's bodies—my four younger brothers and sisters, babies as dark skinned as those people I'd just left on Dover Place.

I held my bare leg out toward the bus aisle to look at the light skin above my loafers, and as if it was yesterday I remembered the time I smeared thick mud from Cutter's Creek all over my feet and legs and sat in the sun until it dried so I'd look like the rest of the kids. Then, just when I was feeling so happy, I was grabbed up and held under the pump and scrubbed while Mom scolded, "Ain't you 'shamed Rosie? Gettin' yo'sef all dirtied up like that? Remember, yo' is white—*keep yo'sef white!* It's what the Good Lord intended!" There were other times she'd change the words of scolding to: "Someday yo' gonna be a fine white lady, Rosie, with fancy clothes and a big white house like Miss Cutters. Yo' is goin' eat off the *fat* of the land and not just get the *scraps!* like poor colored folks got to settle for!"

It was warm on the bus, but a chill went all through me and I started to shake and I couldn't stop. I had to hold my hand over my mouth to keep from retching, because I knew now there was no denying it. I had to accept the fact; they all told the truth tonight. I was colored. I had been made to pass for white. I had lived a lie all these years. I had been denied the love and affection of family life, I had been made to believe I was alone in the world because a woman named Lenora Jefferson decided I should be brought up as white.

Now at eighteen, I relived some of the childhood heartache and once again the tears came as they used to when I'd feel I wasn't loved as much as the others—because I wasn't hugged and kissed like they were—and how I'd hated being different. I realized now Aunt Lottie had my folks prepare me for my lonely parent-less future from the day I was born, because they never said to me like they did to the others, "Come heah to Mama" or "Do this or that fo' Papa." It was always simply "Come heah!" followed by a swat on the behind for nothing, or a box on the ears. I guess they felt I wouldn't miss love and affection if I didn't get any.

After the flashback came the "destiny decision" scene, in which Rosie decides not to tell Bob about herself, but to marry him anyway. Then came obstacle scenes: one in which she consults a doctor about the possibility of her having all white children, or some white and some black. He explains the system of genes to her, suggests she not have children if she wants to be 100 percent safe with her secret. But she knows this would be impossible. She answers the doctor:

"What?" I got to my feet to leave. Suddenly I hated the man. I hated him along with the rest of the world. "But that's why Catholics get married! I've started my instructions already because I feel the same way Bob does. He'd *expect* . . . ."

"Tell me about this Robert Harris. Does he have any strong feelings about—well, how does he feel towards Negroes in general? Everyone at some time or another expresses an opinion about the various races." He added something about it wasn't life's problem that were important, such as mixed marriages and religions, only a human being's attitude towards the problem. Then he waited and I gradually got it all out.

Maybe I said more than I intended, more than I realized, about New Year's Eve, how Bob had teased me—I thought to shock me—about the KKK; what his father thought; how he'd argued with his lifetime friend about the Little Rock situation.

When I finished, the doctor closed the big medical book and sighed, and when he looked at me it was like that night on Dover Place, as if he felt sorry for me, and I wasn't in the mood for pity.

"You've just answered your own questions, Rose. You've got one of two choices: *either give up the idea of marrying your young man now, before it is too late;* or, if you do marry him, make certain *you don't have children.* The decision is yours entirely. Only you, deep down inside, will know which is the right one."

Later in the obligatory scene, (the scene in which the character obligates himself to a future way of life) Rosie has Bob meet the family on Dover Place. She tells him she is a Negro. And that is the end of their romance. The scene with Bob ends like this:

Then, without a word he turned and practically ran back to his car.

My tears blurred my eyes so I couldn't see him, but I heard him gun the motor and pull away with the gears grinding—and I couldn't have felt worse if I'd been under those tires.

Dr. Davis put his arm across my shoulders. "That's not exactly the way I would have handled it, Rose, but tears won't help now. It was a shock for him. Maybe when he has time to think it over he'll call."

I let Dr. Davis talk while he led me into the house, but we both knew Robert Harris would never call.

Next is the conclusion, the *summary*. This area of the story must strengthen the reader's belief that the philosophy that won out, was the right one. For this story, the reader must feel that Rose did the right thing in her hour of "growing up," of maturing.

It took weeks and months of lonely, sleepless nights, and endless heartache to learn to live without him and to convince myself I had done what the Lord expected me to do.

Now, I've finally tucked him away in that corner of my heart reserved for special memories, memories of a world I now look back on as though it was a play I watched from the stage wings, as if some stranger played my part.

I didn't go back to the Elms. Dr. Davis and I were sure Bob had gone to Mrs. Barnes after he left our place, and he convinced me it would be embarrassing for everyone concerned for me to appear. So I wrote Mrs. Barnes a long note, thanking her for the years of love and care she had given me, along with the blunt truth of who I really was. And I never heard from her again, or Amy or Marion. When the carton boxes came with my clothes, I eagerly tore them apart, hoping to find some word of understanding from Mrs. Barnes, but there wasn't any, and I cried with my disappointment. I felt as if I had lost something very special.

I went down to Arkansas that next week. My father had died, but my mother was exactly what I expected her to be, and I was happy to have "found" her—of course, it took days for me to convince her the good Lord didn't intend that parents and children should live in different worlds.

The shack with the newspapers nailed to the windows had been replaced by a decent, modern house after my cousin, Ruthie Mae, married a construction worker.

But what is important, to me anyway, is that I am so at peace, so content with life. Now I feel that I have a purpose for being alive. I am a part of the family at 4817 Dover Place.

Sure, people stare when I walk down the street with Aunt Ellie or Dr. Davis, but I'm getting used to it. So are they, *because they are my folks*, and I've learned to love every one of them. I even feel sorry for those light-skinned colored folks who feel they've got to "pass" as whites to have a good life. I've found it's so much easier, simpler, to live the truth; to know that God had a special place for each one of us; and all we've got to do to be happy is to find that place. So much for Rosie and her problem.

The only problems for the writer, when writing about people of a race different from his own, is to remember that *all of us* cry, laugh, love, hate, and at times all experience fear, greed jealousy. We were all born to die. Most people believe in *a* God, if not the same one, regardless of the color of skin.

12

STORY BREAKDOWN:
My Little Girl's Letter to God

The Confession story market is so extensive and flexible there is a place for stories about almost every personal problem in which a human being may become involved. Heartbreak, failure, disappointments of a hundred types, tragedies from every known cause, faith or lack of it—in God or self or others—all offer material for whatever kind of confession story you want to write, whether it is a true experience of your own or others, or a story that might have been true which you write to sell.

A "family" story with a problem concerning a mother, father and a child is a *love* story, whether the love was long-lasting or of short duration. The child is concrete proof of "sex" in the story.

Whether or not it is a "family" story, it must follow the same basic rules of construction. It must include the same ingredients to bring it to an inspirational conclusion as the teenage love problem; a marital infidelity problem; pre-marital sex, dope addiction, etc.

You say, "Well, you probably *cheated* the reader. You made him think it was going to be an exciting sexy story by using a provocative title!" Or, "The editor used some racy pictures to trap the reader!" You are wrong.

Editors strive for a varied audience. They know those readers who frown on "confession" stories as being too risque for their family will change their minds when they see a story such as "My Little Girl's Letter to God," published in *Personal Romances*. There was nothing misleading about the "blurb" printed below the title, which read: "Oh, the infinite forgiveness of a little child! Maybe God sends them on earth to show us what heaven's really like."

The illustration used by the photography department was not that of a sexy gal in a filmy negligee. It was a small child kneeling in front of her father while he writes the letter she is dictating. The caption reads: "It was as if I was seeing my little girl for the first time, and a strangely wonderful feeling came over me."

This is the story of a married couple who adopt a little girl, Bonnie, when they believe they can not have children of their own. Before the final papers are legalized, the wife does get pregnant and they have a son, Tommy, before Bonnie is a year old.

They live on a farm. A few weeks before Christmas, the mother sees the two children, about five years old, playing at the well. Tommy falls into the well and is drowned. The mother believed she had seen Bonnie shove him before she ran out to warn them away from the well. She blames the little girl for the boy's death. She now resents Bonnie. She wishes secretly it had been Bonnie, and not her own flesh and blood, who drowned.

The *theme* in this story, the point I wanted to prove (remember that there must always be something to prove in every story) is that too often parents wrongfully blame children for things they did not do; that too often parents blame a child without investigating the facts first. They make a snap decision without giving a child the benefit of the doubt.

The *theme vehicle* in this story is Doctor Phillips. Remember that the theme vehicle is the person who acts as the author's mouthpiece and voices the writer's own philosophy.

The story opens with the problem, which is the mother's resentment of Bonnie. Then a flashback is used to let the reader know everything necessary that has happened up to this time. The *obligatory scene* follows, in which the mother comes to realize, matures in her thinking, and picks up where the opening was cut off to continue "onstage" with the present, bringing the story to its conclusion:

The opening:

Saturday morning after Christmas, I kept to the kitchen to escape the holiday smells of drying pine needles, spice cookies, and peppermint candy canes that still clung to the other rooms of our big old farmhouse. Because this had been the first lonely, miserable Christmas I had ever known in all my life. We had lost our four-year-old Tommy just two weeks before Christmas. Along with Tommy had gone my happiness, my ability to love, my desire to live—and yes, my faith in God.

"What'cha doing, Mommy?" Bonnie's small, timid voice came from the doorway.

"Go away! Go away! I hate you!" The words seeped into my thoughts, and to keep from saying them, I silently continued to knead the bread, finding some mental release in the vigorous action of the slap-pat-roll against the dough. For two weeks I had managed to control my tongue, but I knew I couldn't do it forever.

"Can I help you, Mommy?"

I looked up for just a moment, long enough to see her small, pale face with the too-big, too-solemn brown eyes for a child of five. A month ago I would have checked her temperature, worried if she were catching something because of her unnatural paleness and listlessness. But now I ignored her with a quick, "No—I'm in a hurry."

"You used to like me to help. You said once I was the best bread cooker in Fairfield, in the whole world."

Irritable words came to my tongue, but I let them die there. I didn't want to be sharp and nasty to Bonnie. I knew it wouldn't help matters any. I remembered too well what our minister had said once in a sermon: "Children know not when they sin; therefore, we must 'suffer unto us the little children' under all circumstances . . . ."

But I was finding it more difficult every day to talk civilly to the child. Every time I looked at her I thought, why aren't you Tommy? Why did it have to be him, my own flesh and blood? Often I simply ignored her questions, pretending not to hear, and she would walk away.

But now she didn't leave. Without looking I knew she was still there, half leaning against the door frame, her small arms folded across her chest in the grown-up way I used to think was cute.

"Was you ever lonesome, Mommy?"

I banged the bread pans on the table with unncessary noise to hide the effect of her question. What a small word, lonesome, for the immense empty ache inside me, the yearning that was one endless pain—to see a little boy's blond curly head pop out from behind a chair, to hear his boisterous, "Bang! Bang! Don't move! I got ya covered!" as he playfully squirted me with a water pistol.

"Go out and watch your father—he's in the barn," I said fiercely to ease the tremble that rushed through me.

"He's fixin' the tractor—he said I should come in and watch you."

"It isn't too cold. Put your boots on and go outdoors," I insisted. It just won't work that way, Tom, I thought, You can't force me to forgive and forget!

"Okay, Mommy—I'll go outside," she said obediently, and I thought she had gone until she said, "Mommy, is God as smart as Santa Claus?"

This question of Bonnie's is preparation for the conclusion, when she dictates a letter to God. About 1,500 words of flashback follow to tell the reader all he needs to know about Tom and Paula, their desire for a family, how happy they were when they had Tommy, their "miracle" child, how Bonnie was kind and patient to the little boy who was always ailing. In the middle of this section, the reader gets the opportunity to understand the mother, Paula, a little better. It is while she is talking to Doctor Phillips on the phone, telling him to cancel their application for the adoption of a second child.

"Okay, I'll cancel your application. And in case you folks forgot, the final papers on Bonnie haven't been drawn up—you don't have to keep her, you know."

I covered the mouthpiece with my hand and told Tom what the doctor was saying. And immediately I thought, he's right! I don't have to raise a stranger's child. I'll have my own to love. I'll have so many babies there won't be any love to spare.

Tom came over and put his arm around me as he took the phone. "You kidding, Doc? Of course we'll keep Bonnie," he said. "We didn't take her on approval. You know what they say—there's always room for one more."

This remark of Tom's is also a preparation for the conclusion, and is repeated in the summary. The story is brought back onstage, back to the present, to the day Bonnie wanted to help bake the bread and was sent outdoors to play. This is the beginning of the conclusion, and is given to strengthen the reader's understanding of the mother's grief.

When Tom finished his chores at the barn and came in for supper, I went to the window above the sink and looked out for Bonnie. I saw her standing tip-toe on a wooden crate beside the old brick well, balancing herself by her tummy on the edge as she looked down.

Two weeks ago I would have screamed frantically for her to get away from there, but now the words froze on my lips and tears burned my eyes. The swelling that scarcely left my throat these days choked me, making sound impossible.

I had been here like this, helpless, when I saw the two children tussling, when I saw Bonnie grab Tommy's leg. I couldn't hear what she said then, but I had seen the angry, annoyed look on her face those seconds before he disappeared into the well.

My eyes left Bonnie and went to the deep frozen ruts that ran across the yard to the old well, ruts made by the fire department truck that had brought the inhalator, too late. Tom and I had tried frantically for thirty minutes of living, torturous hell to get Tommy out. The water was so cold he cramped and panicked and couldn't do what Tom told him to do.

It hadn't snowed since, and the bare patch was still there, the spot where the snow had melted beneath the blanket and the lifeless little body before he was taken away.

"Supper about ready?" Tom asked from the doorway. "I'll go fetch Bonnie."

When Tom goes out to get Bonnie, there is a second flashback, to tell the reader how Paula's grief affected her feelings toward Tom, and that she feels God has forsaken her.

I no longer accepted his love, his kisses. I ignored the look of helplessness and sympathy in his eyes. Last night when he tried again to take me into his arms, to soothe away my sobs, he said, "Please, Paula, it doesn't help to cry. Remember, he was my son too. I loved him as much as you did."

"But you loved Bonnie more!" I pulled away from him, and things that had been simmering inside of me for days suddenly boiled over. "She was always your favorite. You've still got her. I told you what happened out there, but you don't seem to realize she killed my little boy! She pushed him in!"

"Paula, even if she did, it wouldn't have been deliberately. God knows . . . ."

"Don't talk to me about God!" I cried. "He can't put my baby back in my arms! Oh, I want him so bad, I haven't anyone to love . . . ." I turned to the wall and cried myself to sleep like I did every night, my last waking thought that God had forsaken me.

Supper was more tortured and quiet tonight than it had ever been. I believe it was the quiet I couldn't bear as much as it was seeing the empty place beside Bonnie.

There are about 100 words which get them through supper and Paula's tidying up, until Bonnie says:

"Mommy, I want to write a letter to God."

I turned around. She had a pencil and tablet in her hand. "Go away—go away!" I wanted to cry. Write to God? *Was* there a God?

"I want you to write it, Mommy," she was saying. "Santa Claus can read my writing, but I don't want to take a chance on God and the hard words." I remembered her illegible scribblings to Santa Claus before Christmas, while Tommy was still alive.

I saw Tom through the doorway, rocking fast, his head buried deep in the paper.

"I'm tired, Bonnie. Ask Daddy to do it." I dismissed her, mentally and physically, and sat down at the kitchen table to look at a new magazine.

I don't know when I first became aware of the voices in the front room—Tom's so purposely unemotional, repeating Bonnie's eager, high-pitched words. While I listened, I watched the beads of water come out on the back of my hands as they lay on the table.

"I know it must be awful nice up in heaven, God, 'cause Tommy didn't come back to us for Christmas, so I want to come to heaven, too—you got that, Daddy?" Bonnie stopped to ask.

And Tom simply said, "Yes, I got that."

"I'm awful lonesome for Tommy, God—I got nobody now, and it's a long time till I go to school in September," she went on. "I looked in the well today. I was going to fall in, too, so I could come to heaven, but it's all covered with ice. I don't want to wait till it melts, God. I want to come right now . . . ."

I got up from the chair and went to the doorway. Bonnie was leaning against Tom's rocker, looking at what he was writing. My heart pounded so I thought it would burst. Tom's head was bent, and I couldn't see his face.

She went on, "Mrs. Benson said some people just fall to sleep and go to heaven, so God, tonight when I get to sleep, please see I get to heaven, like it says in 'Now I Lay Me Down to Sleep'—You know the one I mean . . . ."

I just stood there and listened and sucked in the hot tears when they fell to my mouth and felt sick and ashamed. I waited for her to go on, but now she leaned down, the better to look into her father's face. "Daddy," she said, oh so seriously, "Are you sure God sees everything we do?"

"Yes, Bonnie," Tom answered quietly, "He does." And I know he was thinking of what I'd told him about the tussle at the well.

"Then He knows I tried awful hard to hold on to Tommy's leg. I didn't want him to get wet, but he kept pushing my hand away. Daddy, he got so mad! He said no girl had to hold him while he got his airplane that zoomed into the well. I told him we'd better fetch you 'cause he'd fall in and Mommy'd get awful mad if he got wet 'counta his cold. Then he did fall in, and Mommy . . . ."

I couldn't stand it another second. I ran in to them, got down on my knees, and pulled Bonnie into my arms.

Another 500 words follow in which Paula realizes how wrong she has been, and the love and deep-rooted affection between the three of them is restored. This scene ends with them calling Doctor Phillips to arrange for the adoption of another child as soon as possible. (When Tommy was born, surgery was necessary for Paula, making future pregnancies impossible.)

The *summary* includes previous statements by both Tom and Paula:

Tom came down on the floor beside me and took the two of us in his arms, and just as surely as if he could read my mind, he smiled and said, "You know that old saying, kitten—'there's always room for one more!'"

"Or two or three," I added, laughing with him.

Suddenly the tension, the anguish, the heartache that had burdened the three of us these past weeks were released like a spring lock, and although Bonnie didn't understand what was so funny, she laughed with us.

She forgot about her letter the minute she heard us on the phone talking to Doctor Phillips about a "brother for Bonnie." But I will never forget, and I will always thank God for letting me read it—and understand it—in time.

I'm sure Tommy knows I won't ever forget him; that I won't give away the love I had for him. I will just open my heart wider to make room for those children that come my way.

There was nothing unusual or exceptional about the writing in this story. I am sure it made no inroads on the field of literature. Most anyone of you reading this can write a story as well if not better. But it was used as an example to emphasize the fact that *any* family problem can be written into a salable confession magazine story.

13

STORY BREAKDOWN:
I Was Whistle Material

In an earlier chapter I promised to provide a complete break down, by scenes, of a typical confession story. For this I have used my own story "I Was Whistle Material," as published in *True Experiences*.

You may remember that this story concerned a woman who was faced with the removal of a breast because of cancer. Her husband had always admired her shapely figure, laughingly calling her "whistle bait." She is afraid that surgery will disfigure her for life and he will not love her as much, only pity her. The theme to prove was that "beauty *is* only skin deep; it is what is in the heart that matters."

    I WAS WHISTLE MATERIAL *(I DIDN'T WANT PITY!)*

    1. Through my tears I looked at myself in the full-length closet door mirror. 2. Outwardly, I didn't look

any different at twenty-four than I did five years ago when I married Kerry Hopkins. 3. He whistled at me the first time he saw me and he said dozens of times since I was still whistle material; he said he fell in love with my figure before he saw my face!

4. But I wouldn't be "whistle material" without my breasts! 5. I held my hand over the one, then both, trying to imagine what I would look like, but the horrible thought made me shake all over again. 6. Dr. Alpine had said, "maybe both breasts"—maybe he'd have to remove both of my breasts; he wouldn't know until after the pathologist studied the biopsy specimen.

7. The longer I looked the harder I cried—maybe it was just half pity, or because I'd tried not to all day. 8. It just didn't seem possible this time yesterday, I was so happy, the world so right—I was so wrapped up in Kerry's love, a love that might soon turn to *pity*—and oh, dear God, I couldn't stand pity instead of love!

9. My fingers dug into my flesh so hard I winced and cringed, so vividly imagining the scars were already there, I could actually *see* the ugly things. 10. How terrible I would look to Kerry! 11. When he wanted to hug and fondle me, he would probably just smile gently instead, and turn away.

12. Oh, dear Lord, *why?* 13. Why me? 14. I cried over and over. 15. Now that it was too late, I wished I hadn't gone to Dr. Vail; that I hadn't agreed to quit work and raise a family; then I wouldn't have learned this terrible thing. 16. Yes, those minutes standing there in front of that mirror, I felt I'd rather have been ignorant of my condition until it killed me, because death seemed easier to take than the thought of

being a freak for the rest of my life. 17. Does this sound stupid and vain? 18. Maybe so, but that's the way I was; maybe because Kerry and I were still sweethearts, after five years of marriage.

19. Yesterday we were having our usual late lazy Sunday breakfast when Kerry laid his paper down and said, 20. "Well honey, remember what day tomorrow is?"

21. I told him I couldn't recall anyone's birthday, and we'd had our anniversary celebration over a week ago.

22. "It's your three month check up with Dr. Vail; you missed the last one, and its also the day you turn in your resignation, the day you tell them at Wallace s you are quitting, as per agreement with your one and only ever lovin' husband."

23. And then I did remember. 24. We had decided when we got married that I would work only three years, then stay home to start our "planned parenthood" family: at least one boy and one girl. 25. But I had let the three years slip by, then four. 26. I had begged Kerry to let me continue to work until we had enough to pay down on this little house, and I wanted a new washer and dryer.

27. "We've got the house, the new car," he enumerated. 28. Then he came over and put his arms around me. 29. "How's about it, sweetie, ready to be a Ma?" he said, nuzzling me behind the ear.

30. I laughed at his eagerness and reminded him it usually took nine months to have a baby. 31. I had a good job. I was manager of the ladies ready-to-wear at Wallaces, but the more Kerry's question formed in my

mind, the more I liked it, provided I found someone to train to take my place.

32. "Okay, I'll give you two weeks to find a replacement, but at least tell them tomorrow. 33. And keep your appointment with the doc, and have an extra special checkup, sweetie," he added. 34. "You've been working too hard lately. 35. I don't like you having to take so many vitamin pills; we're young, you eat good food, you shouldn't need them," he rambled on and I just listened. 36. I was tired, though it was still morning, and I didn't feel like talking.

37. That was the main reason I didn't argue with him about quitting. 38. I had been feeling bushed for weeks. 39. I thought it was because of the extra work at the store for the sale, and I didn't bother to go to Dr. Vail. 40. I just bought a big jar of super vitamin pills and "ate them like candy," to hear Kerry tell it.

41. We made a real occasion of our decision for me to become a housewife and mother. 42. We dressed up and went out for supper, then went to the Peacock Inn to dance. 43. Kerry flirted with me all evening, and I loved it. 44. I had such a wonderful time, I forgot how tired I was.

45. When we got home I put on the new lace nightie my sister Mable gave me for my anniversary. 46. I had just come into the bedroom when Kerry pulled our calendar with the days marked on it down from the closet door. 47. He smiled and winked his eye at me while he tore it in half. 48. "I never did like making love by the calendar," he said, and I mentally agreed with him. 49. But the "schedule calendar" was part of our planned parenthood arrangement, and we followed

it faithfully, many times wishing we'd never heard of the darn thing.

50. Later, when I settled down to sleep, I snuggled up close to Kerry's arms and gave a silent prayer of thanks to God for giving me such a wonderful husband, for letting me be the happiest girl in the world. 51. I was still glowing in the morning when Kerry kissed me goodbye and reminded me,

52. "No excuses today, honey. 53. Drop everything this noon and keep that appointment with Dr. Vail. 54. We've got to make sure our Mommy's in the pink of condition."

55. Dr. Vail had been our family doctor for as long as I could remember and I guess that's why my visits to him were more or less a friendship session, with him sending me back to the store with a kiss on my cheek, best wishes to Kerry and my sister, and the usual remark not to work so hard; to slow down and have fun; that there were more important things in life than money and new house gadgets.

56. So today, when I told him we took his advice and discovered there *was* something more important than money—babies—and that I wanted to have one as soon as possible, he gave me a hearty bear hug.

57. "Well, young lady, in a case like that, let's really look the situation over," he said, and he acted as pleased as Kerry was at the idea of me being a mother. 58. "Since this young man has been five years in the planning, he's got to be healthy as well as beautiful."

59. He had already given my chest the routine check with his stethoscope, but when I said I wanted to breast-feed my baby the first months, like Mabel

always did, he started to probe around with his fingers pretty thoroughly. 60. After a minute he asked me about the lump he felt, but I told him not to worry, it didn't hurt. 61. It hadn't for years.

62. "You remember that Hansen family I baby-sat for?" 63. I laughed at the memory. 64. "Those kids! 65. If mine turn out like that I'll shoot them!" 66. It was the boy, Timmy, who hit me in the breast with his bat when I tried to break up the baseball game in the living room. 67. Mrs. Hansen had called Dr. Vail, thinking Timmy had broken my ribs, it hurt me so bad. 68. But nothing was broken; my flesh was tender and sore for months, but I was fifteen, that age when a girl is too embarrassed to talk about her body, so I pretended it was all right almost immediately.

69. I rambled on about Mrs. Hansen and I didn't notice Dr. Vail had become so quiet and serious until he pinned me down to specific questions about the bruise: How long it had been tender? When had it stopped hurting? Why hadn't I mentioned it to him before? 70. I told him I had forgotten about it until one night this last winter when I imagined there was a tightness under the flesh. 71. He seemed so annoyed that I hadn't told him that I quickly added, [72.] "But it wasn't a pain, it didn't really hurt, Doctor Vail." 73. Then the blood rushed into my cheeks, remembering that lately when Kerry touched my breasts, I'd sometimes wince with a slight pain.

74. The doctor raised first one arm, then the other, and he was so serious while he probed around that I had to laugh. 75. "Okay, if you think I'll fall apart," I

said, "I'll bottle feed the baby. 76. "Remember, Kerry whistled at my figure long before he saw my face. He declares he doesn't have to waste time looking at other gals as long as I stay the way I am."

77. But Doctor Vail didn't laugh.

78. In fact he didn't say anything more to me until I got ready to leave. 79. "Can you stay a little longer, Mauri?" he asked me. 80. "I'd like Dr. Alpine to examine you. 81. He's a specialist, two floors up."

82. I assumed he meant an obstretics specialist and I reminded him I wasn't pregnant yet; that surely I didn't need special instructions until I had at least had the usual symptoms of pregnancy. 83. But because I knew my baby would be just like a grandchild to this kind, elderly man, I agreed to wait while he went up to get Dr. Alpine.

84. I glanced around me at the rather old-fashioned office. 85. I thought back to the many times I had been there as a little kid with the usual childhood illnesses, long before my parents died and many times after. 86. I don't suppose they had paid for most of the doctor's visits; they never could pay for much of anything. 87. I was one of five children, and hearing the constant bickering over bills that never got paid for the fourteen years before my folks died in a car wreck was one of the reasons I was so determined to work after I was married, so we could pay for the things we wanted.

88. I'd gone to live with Mabel who was married and had three small children of her own. 89. When she could spare me, I took babysitting jobs to buy my

school clothes. 90. Mrs. Hansen used to tell me I should be a model because of my long slim legs, small waist, and high full bosom. 91. But I soon learned it took more than a nice figure and a pretty face to be a professional model; it took time and money, too, that I didn't have. 92. Mrs. Hansen got me the job at Wallace's as a salesgirl my senior year at high school, and modeling ready-to-wear two hours a day on the second floor was as far as I got as a model.

93. There were three of us salesgirls who did this. 94. In winter we walked around among the customers wearing inexpensive fur coats. 95. In the fall we modeled back-to-school sports clothes. 96. And in April, right after the Easter rush, we started the vacation days promotions by modeling bathing suits.

97. That's what I was doing when I met Kerry.

98. That Monday morning I heard his whistle, the kind that automatically makes a girl look around, and I saw the young man up on the stepladder, doing something to the air-conditioning fuse box. 99. He was staring at me over his shoulder while he whistled.

100. I believe I fell in love with Kerry that first minute. 101. Before the week ended, he knew all there was to know about me, and I knew he was twenty-three, going to insurance school at night, working days as a maintenance man for Wallace's, and that he was in love with me, too.

102. I had had dates before Kerry Hopkins, but at nineteen, I was certain I would never have another date with anyone else. 103. And he'd said many times since that he knew from the first glance of my, from up on his stepladder, that I was the one and only girl for him.

104. Whenever he says this, he winks his eye and adds, "It was the shape that got me."

105. I picked up a magazine for mothers-to-be and while I leafed through it, I thought how nice it would be to talk with Mabel about babies, to be one of those gals I'd see pushing a baby in the cart up and down the aisles of the supermarket, and I was all but singing a lullaby when the two doctors came into the room.

106. Five minutes later, my mood to sing was changed to cold fear because of Dr. Alpine's questions and examination.

107. When he finally said I could get dressed, he asked me if I could come in the next day to Cincinnati Memorial Hospital to have the lump removed from my breast. 108. He said it would be a biopsy, a small incision.

109. "I couldn't possibly," I told him. 110. "We're having a big sale at the store; I should be there right now, I'm so late." 111. Then I smiled at the two of them while I finished buttoning my blouse. 112. "Anyway, if that little lump has been there a long time, surely a little longer won't matter, will it?"

113. "I'm afraid so, Maura," Dr. Alpine said. 114. "You've waited a couple of years too long as it is; now every day matters; Dr. Vail will make the necessary hospital arrangements."

115. I was looking in the mirror combing my hair and without turning around I asked him why in the world I would have to go to the hospital for so minor a thing.

116. "I'm not an alarmist, Maura," he began, and something in his voice made me turn around, fast. 117.

"Remember it's the pathologist who gives the final word. 118. But, in my opinion, the small tumor you feel is one of many, and I believe they are malignant."

119. I must have formed the horrible word *cancer* that very minute. 120. I asked him how he could tell by just feeling; it was such a small lump; it didn't hurt; I'd had it for a long time.

121. "Many women get all upset imagining they have cancer when what they have is nothing more than a small cyst that can be lifted out in a matter of minutes. 122. But everything here indicates just the opposite, Maura; your physical condition in general, the shape of the lump, and the small peaks on it and the glands here." 123. He raised my arm to point out the section Dr. Vail had been so concerned with. 124. He explained that after the specimen from the biopsy was given to the pathologist, if Dr. Alpine's suspicions were confirmed, major surgery would have to be done immediately to check the spread of the cancerous cells into my blood. 125. I was to come for the biopsy, prepared to stay at least a month in the hospital.

126. "What do you mean, *major surgery*?" 127. I finally got the question out, almost knowing what his answer would be.

128. "Removal of the breast; I hope just the one, but if it means your life, of course we will do both at the same time." 129. Then while I slowly died a thousand deaths, he talked about the new method of breast surgery, explaining it all in words I could understand, saying there would just be a straight line scar, nothing to be ashamed of.

130. "No! I won't have it done! 131. You're not going to make a freak out of me!" 132. I stared at him in horror, and started for the door. "You're just trying to scare me!" I cried, and I couldn't stop once the words started. 133. "You just want to experiment on me; you want to do another operation! 134. *Well, it won't be on me!*" I said a lot of other things and neither doctor tried to stop me. 135. "It's all just research with you doctors, you don't care about the *person.*" I was yelling and crying at the same time. 137. "Well, forget it, I'm not going to be your guinea pig!" 138. I was in the next room before Dr. Vail reached me. 139. He put his arms around me.

140. "Go ahead, honey, cry; I guess I would too," he said. 141. Then he went on about how I wasn't the only woman who had this done. 142. He tried to reason with me, to explain how lucky I was that Dr. Alpine had discovered it now, before it was too late, and that there was still a long life ahead of me. 143. "You'd be surprised at the number of women who wear special garments and no one knows they've had this operation," he said. 144. And that stopped my crying.

145. "No one knows? I said. 146. "What about . . . ." the vision of Kerry's horrified look, the cringing that would come in his eyes when he'd see my scarred, flat chest, made it impossible for me to say, what about when I'm undressed? 147. What about when my husband wants to make love to me, then turns away because he can't stand the sight of me? What about then?

148. "Talk it over with your husband, Maura," Dr. Alpine said. 149. "He'll understand the wisdom of immediate surgery. 150. He may even suggest your going to several other doctors, and I believe that would be a good thing; just so you do it immediately." 151. Long before he finished, I had made up my mind—*I wouldn't tell Kerry!*

152. I got out my lipstick to fix up a little before going back to work. 153. The specialist must have taken my sudden calm for having "seen the light" and agreed to the surgery, because he went on to say what all would happen if I didn't have it done. 154. I'd have one year, two at the most, to live; cancer was such a treacherous disease it often left its original source and went to some other vital organ of the body; got a foothold before it was discovered; there was no medicine that could ease the pain toward the end, an end that followed months of bedridden invalidism. 155. He told me how fortunate people like me were that there was such a nation-wide cancer program that made it possible for doctors to find this "killer" in time. I just let him talk on and it all went in one ear and out the other.

156. When I was ready to leave, I gave Dr. Vail a quick kiss on the cheek and, glancing at his name plate on the office door, I smiled and said, [151.] "If it's a boy, we'll name it Kerry Henry, for the two nicest men in my life." and before I was halfway down the hall, I had already pretended the noon visit had never happened.

158. I had just gotten back to Wallace's when Kerry called me. 159. Mr. Hudson, the big boss from Tulsa,

was on a tour with three other sales managers, and between flights he wanted Kerry to have dinner with them so they could go over some of the proposed sales campaigns. 160. Occasionally Kerry worked late and he didn't call because he knew I understood, but the main reason he called now was to find out how I felt, and what Dr. Vail thought about us having a baby.

161. "Everything's fine, Kerry," I lied. 162. Then I told him not to work too hard, and sent a kiss to him, too, over the phone.

163. I kept so busy the rest of the day it wasn't hard to keep up the pretense that everything was fine. 164. But when I got home and hung my jacket up in the closet, and saw myself in the full-length door mirror, the full impact of Dr. Alpine's verdict hit me.

165. At first, I bristled with resentment that he could be so casual about such a horrible operation. 166. I couldn't even think of having such a thing done. 167. Not *me*! 168. Not Kerry's pinup girl, his "whistle material."

169. I was so tired, both mentally and physically, I fell on the bed to rest a few minutes. 170. I lay there and I listened to the early evening noises that came in the open window—mostly TV sets blaring westerns or children's programs, and the sounds of the boys on our street playing catch. 171. And all I could think was that some day soon, these same noises would be in my house, in my yard, from my son.

172. It's strange how you can do without something for ages and never miss it, but the day you decide you want or can afford it, you feel you must have it that very minute. That's the way it was now with me and

the idea of being a mother. 173. I lay there and wished there was some miracle by which I could speed up the nine months of pregnancy.

174. I began feeling so good I went in to take a shower, and I hummed lullabies all the while. 175. Later, I settled down to do my nails in front of the TV to keep awake until Kerry got home. 176. When I checked the newspaper for the TV programs, my eye caught the picture of the little girl who had just been granted an audience with the Pope in Rome. 177. She had but a few months to live and that was her last wish.

178. I stared down at the picture, at the article, but other words screamed around in my mind, ",... one year, maybe two; invalided years; no medicine to ease the pain toward the end; you're lucky to have this discovered in time; one year, maybe two . . . ."

179. I was sick to my stomach and perspiration came out on the backs of my hands holding the newspaper, and I hurt all over. 180. How could I have been so stupid not to realize what the doctors were trying to tell me?

181. If I didn't have the surgery I would be an invalid in a year, and die in two—maybe less. 182. Dr. Alpine said to check with other doctors, but he must have been sure his diagnosis was correct or he wouldn't have dared say the things he had.

183. I tried to organize my thoughts, to reason, because I had to accept the one all-important truth—*I couldn't get pregnant, not with cancer in my body.* and I cried over and over, [187] "No! No! *I just can't! I won't be a hideous freak!*"

188. And neither could I have a baby—not now.

189. Then, like a person often does in a confused, frightened mental state, I began to scheme and think all sorts of things. 190. First that maybe the doctors were wrong, maybe it wasn't incurable. 191. Every day new drugs were discovered for various diseases—cancer research had been going on for years. 192. I would wait—everyone with cancer didn't rush into surgery. 193. I'd wait and see. 194. Radium treatments—I had read once that they gave radium treatments for cancer—that's what I would do; I would find a doctor who gave radium treatments. 195. Kerry would never know, not until I was on the was to being cured, *then* I would tell him. 196. And *then* I would have our baby. I would have to find the schedule calendar Kerry had thrown away; I'd have to abide by it, without him knowing it, for a while, and be doubly cautious.

197. I was still there in front of the mirror when Kerry came home and called out. "Hi, honey. [199.] Your Pappy's home. [200.] Come running for that kiss." 201. And my throat got so tight I couldn't answer him. 202. I just ran into his arms and clung to him and let him believe the tears were from happiness, the same happiness he felt, and I knew I couldn't do anything to spoil it.

203. In our bedroom Kerry said all of the nice little things that make me feel so loved, so desired. 204. And most of all, he said, was the pleasure of not having to make love on schedule. 205. But all I could think was—early tomorrow is trash pick-up and I've got to find the Planned Parenthood calendar! 206. I couldn't remember my "safe" days that were marked on it.

207. I got cold and sick inside, lying there trying to think while Kerry pulled me closer. When I mumbled I was tired, he only grew more tender. 208. "Let Doc Kerry make you feel better, sweetheart," he said. 209. For answer I drew away, tried to ease out of his arms, and oh, dear God, what an effort it was.

210. Aloud I begged, [211.] "Please, Karry, not tonight. 212. I'm sorry but I just don't feel—"

213. "Well, okay—" he stopped me. 214. "Never let it be said I took my wife by force." 215. Then, as if sorry for his words, he reached over and kissed my cheek. 216. "That wasn't a nice thing to say, was it? I'm sorry. 217. Guess you've had a big day at the office," he apologized. 218. "And there's always tomorrow." 219. And we both settled down to sleep.

220. But I could tell by his breathing that Kerry lay awake, hurt and puzzled by my behavior. 221. And I lay awake too, with a nervous anxiety to get up, to go out to the trash barrel. 222. The trash truck usually came about six-thirty in the morning while Kerry was dressing, so I had to get it tonight. 223, 224. It seemed like forever before Kerry fell asleep and I knew it was safe to slip out of bed. 225. It took ages to find the calendar, then I took it into the kitchen.

226. I was at the table trying to tape it together when Kerry came to the doorway, then came over to see what I was doing. 227. There was a horrible moment that stretched into eternity before he spoke.

228. "So you didn't mean a word of it?" he declared. 229. "You no more wanted a baby than the man in the moon, did you? 230. It's far more important that you buy all the fancy gadgets you want for

the house than it is to be a mother." 232. He said it all in such a flat, odd tone, I knew there was no use trying to deny or explain, then.

233. "I guess all this waiting," he went on, "all your promises, all of your words about how you couldn't wait to get pregnant, how much you loved me—it was all just words. 234. Maybe you're just in love with that body of yours—don't want to risk changing it. Well, you won't have to worry anymore."

235. "Kerry, I do love you! 236. And I meant everything I said." 237. I wanted him to put his arms around me, to hold me close, while I told him why we had to wait to have our baby. 238. I wanted to tell him what the doctors wanted to do to me, but I couldn't get the horrible words out. 239. So I sat there and he went out, calling from the hall, "Goodnight, Maura. I've got a big day tomorrow," and seconds later I heard the door of the spare room shut—the room that was to be our nursery.

240. I cried most of the night . . . sometimes I'd declare to the dark that I would be cured, that I didn't need surgery. 241. Then, the next minute, I'd see myself in a wheelchair, bedridden, Kerry patient, kind, but filled with pity. 242. Then, like a bolt, it hit me! 243. His pity wasn't because I was ill, but because I had been too blind and foolish—yes, even too vain, to keep myself from being in that wheelchair!

244. That was truly the most horrible time of my life—those hours I lay there and tried to make a decision. 245. A decision to risk death by waiting for some vague miracle, or to be assured of life. 246. Because, as night faded into morning, and I relived

everything Dr. Vail and Dr. Alpine had said; their thorough examinations; the questions they asked, and my answers; I had to admit once and for all that I would have to submit to surgery if I expected to live, *if I wanted to live*. 247. And—if I wanted to keep my husband.

248. I got up and went down the hall to the spare room and knelt down beside the bed in the half light of early dawn. 249. I prayed. 250. "Dear God, help me do this . . . ." 251. Then aloud, I said, [252,] "Kerry, I love you so much." I could tell by his breathing he wasn't asleep, but he didn't answer me. 253. I took a deep long breath to keep my courage, then went on, [254.] "I did go to see Dr. Vail today—but I wasn't honest with you, Kerry. 255. Everything isn't fine." 256. Then I told him. 257. Once started, it wasn't so difficult. 258. With each word, I could feel my heart lighten.

259. He let me finish without interrupting, then he reached up and turned on the lamp beside the bed, and there were tears on his cheeks. 260. Not tears of pity for me . . . I knew that before he said anything. 261. They were tears of sorrow that I had been so foolish as to try to bear this thing alone, that I hadn't asked for his help. 262. "Oh, baby, baby," he said, holding me close, "I love you, don't you know what that means? 263. It's you, the heart and soul of you that I love, not the flesh that covers your body." 264. And he said other things that made me ashamed I hadn't trusted his love enough to share my problem with him.

265. He wouldn't even wait for full daylight, but went in to the phone and called Dr. Vail to tell him to

make the necessary hospital arrangements for as soon as possible.

266. It has been a year and a half since my operation.

267. The pathologist's report was exactly what Dr. Alpine expected it to be. 268. And I was in surgery within the next hour after the biopsy.

269. They only had to remove the one breast.

270. I have a little boy, Kerry, Jr., six months old, and I'm expecting again in the fall. 271. While I write this Kerry is out back fencing in our yard as if just any day now the baby will be out there playing ball.

272. I will have to be honest and say it took a long time for me to get over being self-conscious about myself. 273. Maybe I'm not completely over it, but I don't cry anymore, and Kerry has helped wonderfully to keep my spirits up. 274. Most of our friends, of course, know what I had done, but when I am dressed, it doesn't show—and when I'm not dressed, well, like Kerry says, a "sexy" nightie really does things for a woman, and the fact that one side of me has a special padding doesn't seem to matter at all.

275. The most wonderful thing that resulted from the surgery is the fact that now I feel so good all of the time, even in pregnancy. 276. When I do get tired, it is just a good, plain, old-fashioned sleepiness that needs nothing more to be remedied than a night cuddled close and warm in my husband's arms.

277. Pray? 278. Yes, I always have and always will. 279. It has been said to me, "but prayer didn't help you, Maura, you still needed surgery." 280. And my answer was that my illness was man-made, not God-

made. 281. But the desire to get well, the courage to decide in time the right thing to do—*that* was God-made—and the reason for my prayers of thanks.

The basic theme of "I Didn't Want Pity" is the good old standby, "beauty is only skin deep." This is covered in one of the Ten Commandments: "Thou shalt have no other God but me," or vanity is sinful. The secondary theme is, "better to live with a scar than not to live at all."

The *purpose* for the sentences, or groups of sentences, to show why they were put into the script, and what they were supposed to achieve while working toward a thematic conclusion, follows:

1. To set the mood for the story.

2. Establishes age, sex and marital status of the main characters for the reader.

3. Hints at story problem; i.e., a physical issue. (If this were to be a story about blindness, the eyes would have been mentioned, not the body.)

4—6. The problem is presented (needs surgery).

7—11. Gets reader sympathy.

12—18. To establish the situation of this couple when the problem appears.

19—36. First onstage flashback to firmly establish the situation. Remember, the problem and the situation are two different things. This flashback establishes for the reader a bit more, progressing from 12, and shows the way these two felt about each other before the problem appeared.

37—44. Develops a logical stage for the discovery of Maura's illness, so it is not a sudden jolt or surprise for the reader.

45—50. Given as a logical reason for this couple being childless after five years of marriage.

51—54. Develops more logic to lead into the discovery of Maura's disease.

55—59. Introduces the doctor as a family friend, to act as the story theme vehicle. Remember, in the personal problem story, the theme vehicle is the one who advises, guides, or helps the main character with a problem.

60. Introduces the problem.

61—68. Flashback to plant roots for onstage problem.

69—75. Brings the story back to the present, develops the problem.

76. Repeats, for emphasis, the attitude of these main characters toward each other to give further depth to the story. This sentence is intended to constantly remind the reader *why* Maura is worried about her figure changing. (Always stress the *why* of your character's thinking or behavior.)

77—83. *Underplay* of drama, which prepares the reader for bad news.

84—89. Flashback to give deeper roots to the heroine's character, and further reasoning why this couple remains childless.

99. Develops for the reader the appearance of Maura—to make it more logical why her figure is so important.

91. Develops Maura's character, her personality.

92—96. Stage setting to introduce the romance of the story.

97—104. Flashback to repeat the attitudes of the husband and wife. (Remember,in a love story, see that it has a little love in it!) Develops further the reason the problem seems so magnitudinous to Maura.

105. Back on stage. Builds up tenseness for the reader by showing the heroine's complacence. This technique more or less guarantees the reader that she is about to be jolted out of this complacency.

106—117. Problem development with the crescendo method, slowly mounting to a peak.

118—120. Adding roots to the problem via a general, universal attitude toward this disease.

121. Another theme for the reader, not to be influenced by psychosomatic ills, such as "imagining" one is a victim of cancer.

122—129. Development of the problem.

130—139. Exploiting Maura's philosophy. (There must always be conflicting, opposing philosophies; one for and one against; one called "A" and one called "Z." One or the other must win out. In this story, Maura's philosophy, which we will call "A," is her belief that "to be loveable, desirable, beautiful, a woman must be whole and unscarred."

140—143. Employing the theme vehicle, by having the doctor advise the main character. The theme vehicle usually represents an opposing philosophy and must win the main character around to a different way of thinking. In "I Didn't Want Pity," the doctor's philosophy will be called "Z," and so is that of the husband; i.e., "it is the heart and soul and mind that makes a person beautiful, not just the flesh of the body."

144—147. The main character's philosophy is developed with the development of the problem.

148—157. A destiny decision scene. This is where the central character makes a decision that will, of course, prove to be a wrong one and will have to be reversed in the obligatory scene and the conclusion. The destiny decision scene always adds trouble for the main character. (In this story, the destiny decision scene comes quite late because I used a flashback beginning for the story.)

158—164. Setting the stage in logical order for the big scene to follow.

165—169. Returns to the opening scene which was chosen as a high drama point. This scene was split to keep the reader from knowing the outcome of the story. At this point, the situation and problem are still the same as they were at the opening. Situation: a young married couple very much in love who want to start having a family. Problem: the wife discovers she has an incurable disease.

169. Development of the problem to add additional logic. Maura is overly tired, which is a usual symptom of this disease.

170—173. Introduction of another philosophy for Maura: "Do not wait for the things you want—go out and get them now," evidenced by her working to buy things for the house, rather than get them in stride with her husband's income. Also, builds up the reader's sympathy for her to excuse what she does later.

174—175. More stage setting.

176—184. *Mental* introduction of obligatory scene. Adds depth to the problem by solidly joining it with the situation to show that although the problem remains the same, *the situation has changed.* Now the wife does not want a baby.

185—188. Develops Maura's philosophy, "A woman is only desirable, beautiful and loved if she is whole."

189—196. *Inner conflict scene*, which leads to an obstacle scene or more trouble for Maura because of her destiny decision not to tell her husband about her condition.

197–205. Two philosophies in conflict; development of a *situation change*; more proof that it was wrong for her to have decided not to tell Kerry what the doctor said.

206–222. This sex scene is underplayed (no pantings, blood running hot and cold, no ripping off of clothes, etc.), and is handled as it is to further develop the husband's personality for the reader so that his attitude later toward the problem is more believable; so the reader will feel he honestly has love and not pity for his sick wife.

223–239. This begins the "ramp arena" scene that leads into the obligatory scene; that portion of the story in which Maura vindicates herself, obligates herself to a way of life in which her philosophy, her thinking, is changed permanently.

240–243. Short inner conflict scene is used here as a transition to cover the passage of time.

244–247. The obligatory scene; the continuance of the drama of the big scene in which *conflicting parties*, the situation, problem and theme vehicle are all presented to produce a conclusion, a solution to the problem.

248–265. The obligatory scene continues to a philosophical conclusion for the problem.

266–271. Summary and epilogue, to further develop *proof* for the reader that the solution to the problem was the right solution.

272–274. Maura's philosophy has changed, which was necessary to give this story a *reason for being told*.

275–276. A message to all those readers who are not feeling well to investigate, to find our *why* by getting a medical checkup.

277–281. Additional philosophy to appeal to the *general* mass: "be thankful for what you have rather than pine for what you've lost."

Type this story *without* the numbers and read it again to get the continuity. Keep your typed copy in a folder where you can refer to it later for specific areas. Type no more than 200 words to a page. Compare later with your own finished typed stories.

"I Was Whistle Material" is based on Maura's beautiful body which she did not want changed. True, the "beautiful body" story problem is not exactly a universal one. But since the subject matter was *cancer*, it was acceptable, because cancer is universal. And one purpose here was to make more women aware of the potential for this disease so they will have annual checkups. Also, the reader does not know if Maura weighs 100 pounds or 150 pounds, if she is five-foot-two or five-foot-ten. Each reader can see her as she wants to be. The reader identification comes with each reader seeing Maura with her own preference of color for hair, eyes, and skin.

To follow a rule of craft mentioned earlier, the "villain" in the story is fully described. This is the "killer disease"—cancer.

This story, being based on a *physical* problem, merited approximately 5,000 words. If it were longer, it would have "dragged." Stories with physical handicap problems should also be about this length.

14

CONFESSION STORY MARKETS

To compile the following listings of leading confession magazines the author interviewed many of their editors regarding the kinds of stories most likely to be acceptable from free-lance writers. Each contributed comments on general requirements for their particular magazines. These have been somewhat condensed here for easy reference.

Confidential Confessions

Dauntless Books
17 E. 44th St.
New York, N.Y. 10036

Editor: Jean Sharbel

Length: 2,000 to 10,000 words
Payment: 3 cents per word on acceptance

Buys all types of first-person stories dealing with teenage courtship, older courtship, young married problems, family problems of all kinds, and stories offering basic inspiration. Prefer feminine viewpoint but regularly use one or two stories from the male viewpoint. All stories must reflect present day life in the wage-earner category; be dramatic and well plotted with no hackneyed situations. Every story should contain reader identification and a meaningful "moral", realized through the narrator's growing maturity and deeper understanding of values. A wide open market for new writers. Offers editorial advice and encouragement when needed. Reports and pays promptly.

Daring Romances

> Dauntless Books
> 17 E. 44th St.
> New York, N.Y. 10036

> Editor: Jean Sharbel

More or less the same information applies to this market since it is one of several magazines Dauntless publishes. The only special requirement here might be a stronger note of adventure and daring along with other emotional factors.

Exciting Confessions

> Dauntless Books
> 17 E. 44th St.
> New York, N.Y. 10036

> Editor: Jean Sharbel

> Same general requirements as detailed for *Confidential Confessions*.

Intimate Story

> Ideal Publishing Corp.
> 295 Madison Ave.
> New York, N.Y. 10017

> Editor: Bessie Love

> Length: 3,000 to 5,000 words (generally)
> Payment: 3 cents per word on acceptance

Buys eleven stories each month dealing with joys and sorrows of everyday kind of people. Particularly interested in teenage problems and ambitions with love interest dominating most stories, although some parent-child relationship stories are bought. Themes and story material must be honest and sincere with no witchcraft, drug-oriented or communal living sequences; have strong emotional crises with concluding moral achieved by character change in narrator through clearer understanding of life values.

Modern Romances

> Dell Publishing Co.
> 750 Third Ave.
> New York, N.Y. 10017

> Editor: Henry P. Malmgreen

> Length: Maximum 7,000 words. No two-parters.
> Payment: 4 cents per word on first two sales; 5 cents per word thereafter on acceptance.

Wide open market for free-lance writers. Beginning authors receive the same careful consideration as those who have contributed many previous stories. Rejects are given brief to-the-point constructive criticisms for revision or for future stories. Uses unhackneyed first-person stories, with high emotional and action suspense with which readers can identify. Themes should deal with today's youth problems and drives, with solutions based on the narrator's greater awareness of moral values.

My Confessions

> Atlas Magazines, Inc.
> 655 Madison Ave.
> New York, N.Y. 10017

> Editor: Jean Robbins

> Length: 6,500 words (average)
> Payment: 3 cents per word on acceptance

Uses all types of human-experience stories in the confession category. General requirements the same as listed for other confession markets.

Personal Romances

> Ideal Publishing Co.
> 295 Madison Ave.
> New York, N.Y. 10017

> Editor: Johanna Roman Smith

> Length: 1,500 to 7,000 words; prefer 3,000 to 5,000 words generally.
> Payment: 3 cents per word on publication. Minimum, $50.00 for shorts.

Uses realistic modern confession stories with strong sex themes and family conflicts involving teenagers, singles and young marrieds' problems and emotional drives. Stories must have emotional impact and action with which readers can identify readily. Good plots and convincing development.

Real Confessions

315 Park Ave. South
New York, N.Y. 10010

Editor: Ruth Beck

Length: 3,000 to 5,000 words (generally).
Payment: Prevailing rates on acceptance.

Uses first-person, female-narrated stories with strong timely themes. Require exciting action-filled plots convincingly developed. Authentic backgrounds with realistic characterizations and plenty of dialogue. Themes should center on romance, marriage problems, parent-child relations, in-law disagreements, with emotional impact, suspense, pathos and understanding.

Revealing Romances

Dauntless Books
17 E. 44th St.
New York, N.Y. 10036

Editor: Jean Sharbel

Length: 2,000 to 10,000 words
Payment: 3 cents per word on acceptance

Same general requirements as detailed for *Confidential Confessions.*

Secrets

Dauntless Books, Inc.
17 E. 44th St.
New York, N.Y. 10036

Editor: Jean Sharbel

Same general requirements as detailed for *Confidential Confessions.*

Tan

Johnson Bros. Pub. Co.
1820 S. Michigan Ave.
Chicago, Ill.

Editor: John H. Johnson

Length: Approx. 5,000 words
Payment: Prevailing rates for top quality stories.

Monthly magazine primarily edited for black readers. Use stories dealing with today's problems involving teenagers and young marrieds in modern life; romance, sexual encounters, parent-child relations. Must be strongly plotted and carefully developed to honestly depict emotional and racial drives in the black world.

Thrilling Confessions

Ideal Publishing Co.
295 Madison Ave.
New York, N.Y. 10017

Editor: Hilda Wright

Length: 5,000 to 6,500 words (generally)
Payment: 3 cents per word on acceptance.

(See requirements listed for other Ideal publications.)

True Confessions

Macfadden-Bartell Corp.
205 E. 42nd St.
New York, N.Y. 10017

Editor: Florence J. Moriarty

Length: 5,000 to 6,500 words
Length: Up to 8,000 words, prefer about 6,500 words.
Payment: 5 cents per word on acceptance.

This monthly magazine is edited primarily for young wives and blue collar families. Most stories accepted come from free-lance writers. Backgrounds and themes should be contemporary, dealing with meaningful and emotionally strong problems with satisfying conclusions. Prefer woman-narrated stories with main character significantly involved in emotional decisions or suspenseful action.

Secret Romances

Dauntless Books
17 E. 44th St.
New York, N.Y. 10036

Editor: Jean Sharbel

Length: 200 to 10,000 words
Payment: 3 cents per word on acceptance

(Same general requirement detailed for other Dauntless magazines.)

True Experiences

Macfadden-Bartell Corp.
205 E. 42nd St.
New York, N.Y. 10017

Editor: Frank Gould

Length: 1,500 to 8,500 words
Payment: 5 cents per word on acceptance. Special payments for short-shorts.

(Requirements much the same as for *True Confessions*.)

True Love

Macfadden-Bartell Corp
205 E. 42nd St.
New York, N.Y. 10017

Editor: Bruce Elliott
Length: 3000 to 6000 words
Payment: 3 cents per word on acceptance.

Uses stories which appeal particularly to young married and unmarried women. Realism and modern backgrounds as well as current attitudes toward life, love, sex and problems involving these emotions.

True Romance

Macfadden-Bartell Corp.
205 E. 42nd St.
New York, N.Y. 10017

Editor: Jean Press Silberg
Length: 6000 to 8000 words; also buy short features 1500 to 3500 words for regular columns.
Payment: 3 to 5 cents per word on acceptance.

Same general requirements as for *True Story*.

True Story

Macfadden-Bartell Corp.
205 E. 42nd St.
New York, N.Y. 10017
Editor: Suzanne Hilliard
Length: 1500 to 8500 words.
Payment: 5 cents per word on acceptance. Special payment for short-shorts.

Monthly magazine edited primarily for blue-collar individuals and families. Ages of main characters may cover a wide range, but late teenagers are preferred. Stories may run the gamut of human emotional problems: young love, courtship, marriage, child-conflicts, frustrated romance, divorce and problems created because of tragic illnesses. Obviously all stories should be provocative, convincing in background and plot development with sex handled realistically but without over-emphasis on sensationalism. All narrators need not be women. Man-told stories are used frequently. Variety is one of the dominant features of this confession magazine. An open-market for new writers who have studied the magazine and learned to handle plotting and strong characterizations.

No attempt has been made to list every possible market for first-person stories. Many general magazines frequently use fiction or articles dealing with personal experiences related by the one who experienced the events. Such stories may run the gamut of human emotion and adventure but the handling of them is somewhat more stylistic. Therefore only those magazines have been listed which make up a comprehensive guide to prevailing markets for the average free lance writer in the confession-story category. These have been listed alphabetically for the reader's convenience but does not necessarily infer that one market is better than another. Editors, the length of stories needed and the prices paid, may change from time to time. It is best to check a current issue of any magazine to which you intend to submit stories before mailing them.

All these magazines list the names of their editors and where to submit manuscripts in the front pages (usually on the index page) of each magazine. If you aspire to writing for any of these markets it is always well to study the magazine carefully before you start the particular story you wish to submit, and to make note of the name of the editor to whom manuscripts are to be sent.

Before mailing your manuscript it is well to double-check to make sure you have properly handled the various elements which will make it an acceptable story. Ask yourself the following questions:

    1—Can the theme be defined in one sentence? That is, what the story intends to prove.

    2—Did I prove what I promised I would prove?

    3—Did I promise something in the opening of the story that I did not deliver?

    4—Is the opening too slow, or have I tried to tell too much at that point?

(The test of this question is whether the reader can guess or anticipate the ending before it is reached. If you feel that is a possibility, then transpose the "revealing statements" to a later part of the story.)

5—Have I presented two conflicting philosophies? If so, is my winning philosophy one which the reader will recognize and accèpt?

6—Have I presented the problem of the story strongly enough in the first 500 words?

7—Have all the main characters been introduced within the first 1,000 words? (This applies to a short story of about 6,000 words. Characters may be introduced who do not become part of the story action until much later in the story.)

8—Have I completed each scene with definite purpose? Have I left any scenes "hanging" without creating proper suspense?

9—Have I used unnecessary scenes merely to introduce a character when narrative would have served the purpose more effectively?

10—Have I accounted for all the main characters in the obligatory scene? (Don't leave the reader wondering what happened to one of the characters who had the limelight in any scene.)

11—Have I built up false suspense, drama, intrigue, or mystery at any point in the story? (If you feel you have then tone down the event or dialogue that created the falseness.)

12—Have I overworked qualifying words, used too many a's, the's, and's; or used two adjectives where one strong adjective would have served; or used adverbs which are too strong for a particular situation? Have I used too much punctuation or too little?

13—Can I honestly feel that I have told my story well and followed the rules editors require in acceptable stories?

14—Can I honestly feel that this is a story properly and well told which a reader will find interesting, exciting or emotional, meaningful, and will want to finish once he starts reading? (If you don't feel that way about your story, go over it again and again if necessary, check the rules which you have studied and make sure you have followed them with strength and creative imagination.)

These fourteen probing questions should enable you to judge your story fairly before selecting the editor to whom you will send it. A little more care at the outset often can prevent a rejection. But be fair with yourself also. Don't be overly critical; and by all means don't keep revising the story needlessly until what may have been interesting and exciting turns into dullness or confusion. If you honestly feel you can improve the story, make your main characters "come alive" more effectively, and better prove the point of the story by some revision, then review the rules for handling these points. Check your scenes against these rules, and determine what real improvement can or should be made.

There are always several ways a scene may be presented, a character introduced, a dramatic incident portrayed, and the details of a story effectively handled. This variety of choice is what makes one writer different from another;

also makes each writer's story different from the same general story told by other writers. Learning to judge your own work will give you confidence in yourself and help you to develop your writing talents to professional standards.

You will also earn the respect of editors. Nothing so quickly turns off an editor's interest as a manuscript which is carelessly handled. And few things brighten an editor's day as much as discovering a new writer with obvious talent. For if the talent is there most confession magazine editors will take time to point out any shortcomings in the story and make revision suggestions.

One fault most beginning writers have is a tendency to digress from the main points of the story he or she wants to tell. Selecting the material which rightly belongs in the story is the first rule of procedure. We have discussed this rule earlier, but it bears reviewing frequently.